FOREWORD BY JOHN C. MAXWELL

THE
33
LAWS OF
STEWARDSHIP

Principles for a Life of True Fulfillment

DAVE SUTHERLAND
KIRK NOWERY

Published by Spire Resources Inc.
PO Box 180, Camarillo, CA 93011
1-800-992-3060

Cover and text design by Bill Thielker

Printed in the United States of America

ISBN 0-9715828-1-5

THE 33 LAWS OF STEWARDSHIP

FOREWORD

I'm a firm believer in the power of principles. When irrefutable truths are put into practice, the impact is deep and lasting, and often life-changing. I have witnessed this countless times with innumerable people from all walks of life on every continent of the world. Principles have an undeniable capacity to transform our thinking and crystallize our priorities, and this fact more than any other has motivated me to write several books on this subject. Two in particular — *The 21 Irrefutable Laws of Leadership* and *The 17 Indisputable Laws of Teamwork* — express a philosophy that is unreservedly based upon biblical ideals. These are not man-made opinions but God-given precepts. Whether we call them principles or standards or laws, they are timeless truths upon which we can base our decisions in every dimension of life.

Two of my closest friends and colleagues, Dave Sutherland and Kirk Nowery, have now created a book which I consider a perfect complement to my own writings. *The 33 Laws of Stewardship* is one of the most compelling, engaging works I have ever encountered on this topic. It is an insightful approach to a challenge each of us faces every day: how to steward the resources entrusted to us by God.

During my 25 years as a senior pastor I spent a lot of time searching for stewardship materials. Most of those searches were futile, and I became burdened by the need to develop stewardship resources and to assist churches in meeting the challenge of capital funding. That led to the establishment of INJOY Stewardship Services (ISS), a ministry which to-date has partnered with thousands of congregations to raise billions of dollars for ministry projects. At the helm of ISS is Dave Sutherland, a man of extraordinary skill and insight. Like a masterful coach, he has directed a remarkable team effort, transforming ISS into a dynamic, multi-faceted service to churches. Working in tandem with him is Kirk Nowery, Executive Vice President of ISS, whom I liken to a multi-talented quarterback who executes every play with true precision. Dave and Kirk, in their interaction with literally thousands of church leaders, have gained an encyclopedic knowledge of stewardship. They know the subject practically, personally and biblically. And now they've distilled that knowledge into this valuable book.

The 33 Laws of Stewardship is an exceedingly practical book. Every chapter is incisive and insightful, zeroing in on a specific principle and bringing it to life. These dynamic pages provide perspectives that are certain to benefit any person who seeks truth and pursues excellence. Although each Law is distinctive, all 33 are relevant to one another. The book's rich combination of biblical examples, poignant illustrations and memorable prose creates a powerful package. Each chapter concludes with a section entitled Living the Laws, which summarizes the principle and translates it into real-life applications. This is truly a valuable component because it moves the reader from ideas into concrete action.

Perhaps the most significant quality of *The 33 Laws of Stewardship* is that it takes a whole-life view of this subject. Stewardship, after all, isn't just about money. It touches virtually every aspect of life and everything God puts into our hands. It is all-encompassing, and the Christian steward's constant challenge is to make the most of every resource. Read this book and you'll learn how to do that with true excellence. I believe you'll also be blessed by the deep devotional quality in these writings because *The 33 Laws of Stewardship* is really like a series of essays on essential, Christ-centered living. I could not commend a book more highly, and I trust it will benefit you as a steward and enrich your life with wisdom. May God bless you richly from the principles that fill these pages.

John C. Maxwell
Founder, INJOY Stewardship Services
Atlanta, Georgia

1

THE LAW OF RIGHTFUL OWNERSHIP

Nothing truly belongs to us;
everything actually belongs to God.

Perspective governs life in remarkable ways. Consider the story of the blind man who attempted to describe an elephant. He put his arms around one of the animal's massive legs and said, "the bark is very rough." He felt the tusk and said, "the branches are smooth but strong." Finally, he handled the giant ear and remarked, "the elephant's leaves are huge and thick." In conclusion he declared, "the elephant is one of the world's most unusual trees."

Lest we laugh at the blind man's misperception, let's remember that we too can get things very wrong at times. Even those of us who have learned that God owns everything often act as if He really doesn't. The first indisputable Law of Stewardship is the Law of Rightful Ownership, which says, *Nothing truly belongs to us; everything actually belongs to God.* King David acknowledged this when he stated categorically: "everything in heaven and earth is yours, O Lord." And he adds right after that statement, "wealth and honor come from you; you are the ruler of all things."[1]

When we are blessed with money and material things, and when we receive acclaim for any accomplishment, we're getting not what we deserve but what God in His grace lovingly allows us to enjoy and to care for. The essence of life is not ownership but stewardship — the faithful management of all that God entrusts to us. Some of us are entrusted with a lot, some with a little; but whatever comes to us brings with it an undeniable responsibility. The temptation is to think that abundance is found in possessing life's benefits, when actually it's discovered in stewarding life's blessings. That's why Jesus warned His disciples: "Be on your guard against all kinds of greed, for a man's life does not consist in the abundance of his possessions."[2] There is only one rightful owner, and true satisfaction comes to us only in acknowledging Him and wisely managing His resources.

> The temptation is to think that abundance is found in possessing life's benefits, when actually it's discovered in stewarding life's blessings.

In what ways can we put this truth into practice? Obviously this is a tough task since the stewardship mindset is so at odds with the prevailing North American attitude of ownership. Nearly everyone falls prey to the notion that life is more fulfilling if we simply have more things. Under the constant barrage of advertisements and appeals it's easy to give in to the belief that we deserve everything we can get. But it's not true, and we run a major risk when we look at life in terms of *our* things, *our* money, *our* possessions, *our* abilities, *our* opinions or *our* achievements. As the Bible says, "we brought nothing into this world, and it is certain we can carry nothing out."[3] You'll never see a hearse pulling a U-Haul trailer.

John D. Rockefeller, America's first oil baron, was the richest man in the world. In the early years of the 20th century, his businesses accounted for one of every thirty dollars generated in the entire United States economy. In today's currency that would be equal to a fortune ten times greater than Bill Gates has amassed. When Rockefeller died in 1937 a newspaper artist drew a cartoon which posed the question, "How much did he leave?" The answer in the next panel said simply, "He left it all." And that's the way it is for everyone. At the moment of death, every "possession" of this material life is left behind — even the bodies we once inhabited. Only the spirit lives on, for only the spirit is eternal.

The "real" reality is found not in the physical world, but the spiritual. That's why Paul told Timothy that "physical exercise is of some value, but godliness has value for all things, holding promise for both the present life and the life to come."[4] Understanding the "real" reality, the Christian steward is able to see life from God's perspective, setting affections and attentions on an entirely different realm — the spiritual realm.

LIVING THE LAWS

As you live out this first Law of Stewardship, let your thinking be guided by three priorities:

Think of yourself as the manager of a trust. You have been given a key role and a great responsibility, so make the most of it. God Himself has entrusted you with time, money, material things and great opportunities. Your objective is to maximize the investment of all that has been put into your hands.

Think of each day as an opportunity for service and stewardship. Time is a precious commodity and we have a limited allotment of days, hours and minutes. Ephesians 5:15-16 advises, "Be very careful, then, how you live — not as unwise but as wise, making the most of every opportunity." It's similar to the popular motto, *carpe diem*, the Latin admonition to "seize the day." But the believer's motto is actually *carpe diem por deo* — "seize the day for God." In other words, live every day expressly for His glory and His purposes.

Think of money as a means to an end, not the end itself. The allure of money is strong and pervasive. It permeates our frantic, workaholic culture; but it brings no lasting fulfillment. It always creates a thirst for more, unless one has the right attitude toward it and determines to manage it rather than be manipulated by it. In the final analysis, the hallmark of stewardship is administration not acquisition. Only by pursuing the goal of pleasing God do we find true pleasure and satisfaction for ourselves.

Scripture References:
[1] 1 Chronicles 29:11
[2] Luke 12:15
[3] 1 Timothy 6:7
[4] 1 Timothy 4:8

2

THE LAW OF PURPOSEFUL POSSESSION

Wise stewards are guided by lordship,
not "hoardship."

The old man had lived in the run-down house for longer than anyone could remember. It was rumored that he had claimed squatter's rights years ago, and the legal owners never contested his claim. From time to time, he shuffled about the neighborhood, pushing a wobbly grocery cart as he searched for discarded treasures. Regardless of the season, he was always dressed in the same tattered clothes. When weeks had passed without a sign of him, someone called the police to report his absence. Upon investigating, the officers discovered his cold, lifeless body. According to the coroner, he had died of starvation.

After the old man's death, nearby residents petitioned the city to demolish the unsightly house where he had lived for so long. The official records were searched and it was discovered that he was not a squatter, after all. He had purchased the house and owned it free and clear. But no heirs could be identified and located, and the demolition order was given. When workers began to dismantle the house, they were startled to find the oddest "insulation" stuffed into the walls, under the floors and crammed into nooks and crevices throughout the structure: authentic stock certificates and other securities worth millions of dollars. The recluse who had lived in abject poverty for years actually had great riches. And, though he could afford the finest food, he ended up starving to death.

The old man was rich in possessions, yet utterly poor because he did not use what was in his hands. He was wealthy, but he gained no advantage from his wealth. Strangely but deliberately, he hoarded the things that could have made his life totally different. As a steward he failed miserably, neglecting the phenomenal resources at his disposal. His pitiful life reminds us of a poignant lesson: worth is gained in what we use, not in what we hold.

On one occasion when Jesus was teaching, a huge number of people gathered around Him. Someone in the enormous crowd yelled out, "Teacher, tell my brother to divide the inheritance with me." Seizing on the man's request, Jesus replied, "Who appointed me a judge or an arbiter between you?" Then, turning to the crowd, He said, "Watch out! Be on your guard against all kinds of greed; a man's life does not consist in the abundance of his possessions."[1]

These are convicting words, especially in a society like ours which is so obsessed with striving to amass as much as possible. It can be truthfully said of Americans that never before in human history have so many people had so many things. Yet we often want even more, and we wear ourselves out to get whatever is next on our list. This kind of self-satisfying behavior is greed, the very thing that Jesus warned against.

To that boisterous crowd of thousands, Jesus amplified the warning by telling the parable of a rich man whose fields produced an excellent crop: Upon seeing his bounty, the man thought to himself, "What shall I do? I have no place to store my crops." So he said, "This is what I'll do. I will tear down my barns and build bigger ones, and there I will store all my grain and my goods. And I'll say to myself, 'You have plenty of good things laid up for many years. Take life easy; eat, drink and be merry.'" But then something dreadful happened. As Jesus explained, "God said to him, 'You fool! This very night your life will be demanded from you. Then who will get what you have prepared for yourself?'" As His listeners absorbed the impact of the story, Jesus drew the parallel: "This is how it will be with anyone who stores up things for himself but is not rich toward God."[2]

> How can we be rich toward God? The answer to this question is of inestimable value because it can lead to the fullest life one can possibly experience.

Let's not miss the meaning of this sobering story. First, where did the man go wrong? He was already rich, and he saw that he was getting even richer. Life had presented him with an extraordinary blessing: a crop so abundant that he didn't have room to contain it. In the midst of this opportunity he asked an important question: What shall I do? But he arrived at the worst possible conclusion: I'll keep it all to myself and I'll live off of it for years. He saw the bounty as something to benefit himself exclusively. It was not to be shared, not to be used for any purpose other than his own pleasure. In exuberant self-indulgence, he promised himself a long, extravagant life filled with eating, drinking and making merry. But it was not to be.

The rich man was a fool, for he had fallen into the trap of prideful arrogance. He thought that his riches were actually *his* riches, when in fact they were on loan to him from God. He thought that the amazing crop was something he deserved, failing to see that it resulted from factors completely in God's control, not his own. He thought that the future was his to predict, willfully boasting of something known only to God. At every turn, he took God's place and denied His authority. He was more concerned with "hoardship" than lordship.

LIVING THE LAWS

The most profound truths in this parable center on one question: *How can we be rich toward God?* The answer to this question is of inestimable value because it can lead to the fullest life one can possibly experience. It is not something mysterious, unattainable or extraordinary. In fact, as the Chinese martyr Watchman Nee once wrote, it is "the normal Christian life."

As you live out this Law of Purposeful Possession, keep these thoughts in mind:

Richness toward God comes through seeing everything as a gift from His hand. Whatever we receive in money or material goods or opportunities or in the moments of each day is purely and simply a gift from God. It's an expression of His love, an evidence of His grace. Every possession is entrusted to us to steward and enjoy and use for His purposes.

Richness toward God comes through seeking His direction before settling on decisions. This is the essence of seeking first the kingdom of God and His righteousness, desiring above all else to do His will.[3] The seeking happens continually as we commune with God and communicate with Him throughout the day. And, whenever we receive "windfall" blessings, the first order of business is to ask, *"Lord, what is your purpose in this? What do you want me to do?"*

Richness toward God comes through caring more about giving than getting. The rich man of the parable was consumed with greed and he cared nothing about giving. And lest we condemn him, let us remember that every person has the same capacity for the same sin. The challenge is to think inclusively about others instead of exclusively about ourselves, for in so doing we grow rich toward God and satisfied in His pleasure. Generously giving at every opportunity, we fulfill our purpose and honor His name.

Scripture References:
[1] Luke 12:13-15
[2] Luke 12:16-21
[3] Matthew 6:33

3

THE LAW OF
MIRACULOUS MULTIPLICATION

*The economics of stewardship is governed
by the mathematics of the supernatural.*

George Müller hadn't faced a situation quite like it. Before him were 120 orphans, expectantly seated at long dinner tables. But something at this mealtime tested the mettle of Müller's heart. On the dinner plates at that table was nothing but crusts of bread. Eager faces looked toward him, as if to say, "What's for dinner?" But he didn't know; the cupboard was bare and the icebox was empty. There was no milk, and no money to buy food or drink.

What was George to do? It didn't take long for him to decide. He would do what he had done every other mealtime. He would instruct the children to bow their heads and join him in thanking God for the meal they were about to eat. He would praise God for the faithfulness of His provision. And so he did. Müller prayed simply, directly, and with a heart filled with faith.

When the "amen" was pronounced, the plates still had nothing but bread crusts. But as the eyes of those 120 youngsters turned again to the head table, a knock sounded at the door. One of the boys was sent to answer. A moment later, he called out, "Mr. Müller, it's the vegetable man! He's got a lot of stuff for us!" "Coincidentally," there were many vegetables that would spoil if he didn't do something with them. While the vegetables were being unloaded, another person came to the door — the butcher! He had run out of ice at the end of a hot day and faced the prospect of awful, rotting meat. Could the orphanage use it? No sooner had he spoken the words than another amazing "coincidence" occurred. The milkman's wagon pulled up, overloaded with milk and dairy products and needing desperately to do something with them!

> They had just seen the evidence of a spiritual law at work – the Law of Miraculous Multiplication. God had transformed their measly bread crusts into the best meal they had ever enjoyed.

Needless to say, it was quite a banquet that night. And it was the finest lesson in faith those orphans ever received. They had just seen the evidence of a spiritual law at work — the Law of Miraculous Multiplication. God had transformed their measly bread crusts into the best meal they had ever enjoyed. He had honored their simple faith with a supernatural supply.

Would the same thing have happened had Müller not prayed, believing God for His provision ahead of time for it? We don't know, but we do know that Jesus said we have not because we ask not. And we know that His will for us is to walk by faith, not by sight.

This raises several crucial questions: In the realm of

stewardship, what does it mean to walk by faith? How can we believe God above and beyond our ability, our resources and our strength? In what ways can we trust Him to provide supernaturally on our behalf?

It's clear from Scripture that the faith-driven life is the life God intends for us. In fact, "without faith it is impossible to please God."[1] Trusting Him explicitly, He provides for us absolutely; and we mustn't be limited by what we see because His ways transcend human understanding. As the prophet Isaiah explained, His thoughts are above our thoughts, and His ways are above our ways.

LIVING THE LAWS

Living the Law of Miraculous Multiplication requires confidence, obedience and courage:

When faced with a major need, express confidence in the Need-meeter. This applies especially when you don't comprehend God's purposes at work. Like Abraham of old, who put his own son on an altar as a sacrifice to God, we must rely on the One who is eminently able. We may wonder, what could we possibly have in common with Abraham? The truth is, many things! As God spoke to Abraham, He speaks to us. As God called Abraham to a life of obedience, He calls us. As God tested Abraham, He tests us. As God called Abraham to a life of faith, so He calls you and me.

When faced with a major need, follow the directions. In order to tap the endless resources of God, the believer must exercise faith by acting in obedience to God's Word. As the Apostle Paul explained to the Romans, "faith comes by hearing, and hearing by the Word of God."[2] When one is prompted by the Word of God or by the leadership of the Spirit, obedience to that prompting is an expression of faith. Such a response enables one to enter into partnership with God, and gives the assurance of success even though the end may not be in sight.

When faced with a major need, brace for a great adventure. The life of faith-filled stewardship is anything but boring. Look at the amazing experiences of those in the "Hall of Faith" of Hebrews 11. Noah, for example, had never experienced a flood nor had he even seen rain, yet he obeyed with regard only for the Lord. Since the command of God came without a specific schedule, Noah had to believe and act accordingly because faith has no time limit. Faith was the only reasonable response for Noah, as it is for us as stewards today.

Scripture References:
[1] Hebrews 11:6
[2] Romans 10:12

4

THE LAW OF
GUARANTEED RETURN
As you give so it will be given to you.

I t was the most outrageously expensive round-trip ticket ever sold, nearly ten thousand dollars to sail from England to America and back. In an era when the average working man made six dollars per week, ten thousand dollars was unthinkable. But a handful of the mega-rich were more than ready to pay such an outlandish sum. In fact, there was a less-than-friendly competition to purchase the few First Class tickets available. After all, this was no typical seafaring venture: it was the maiden voyage of the greatest ship ever built, the *RMS Titanic.*

In April, 1912, the *Titanic* departed from Southampton, England, bound for New York City. She was an impressive sight, a vessel 882 feet long, the length of nearly three football fields. Her width was 92 feet and her eight decks rose to the height of an 11-story building. The *Titanic* had a double-bottomed hull, divided into sixteen watertight compartments. Because as many as four of these could be completely flooded without endangering the ship's buoyancy, the *Titanic* was considered unsinkable.

On the fateful night of April 14, shortly before midnight, the great liner was steaming full-speed through foggy weather when it collided with a massive iceberg. The impact left the *Titanic* mortally wounded, a 300-foot gash ripped in her right side, five of her watertight compartments ruptured and engulfed. The ship thought unsinkable rapidly disappeared into the icy depths, claiming 1,513 lives. Although there were 2,224 passengers aboard, the *Titanic* carried lifeboats for only half that number, and many of them rescued but a handful of people. The list of victims included nearly all of those who paid so handsomely for First Class tickets. For them, there would be no round-trip excursion. The journey was over, and all the money in the world could not purchase their safety.

The *Titanic's* owners boasted that their ship was unsinkable. To those who held round-trip tickets they promised a safe passage and a guaranteed return. But it was a promise they couldn't keep, a guarantee they couldn't fulfill. What seemed like such a sure thing wasn't sure at all; and what appeared to be so safe was actually quite susceptible. The passengers had taken one look at that enormous liner and accepted the promises at face value, never imagining that their confidence would be so tragically shattered.

Life is more like a moving iceberg than a firm bedrock. It's constantly shifting, ever altering, and things are often different from what they appear. There are "sure" promises that can't be fulfilled, "absolute" certainties that turn out to be very, very uncertain. There are "positive" investments that never pay off, "stable" opportunities that degenerate into instability. So what's a person to do? Where do we put our confidence? Whom do we trust? The starting point is to realize that the strength of a promise is dependent upon the source of the promise; and the only ones with real weight are those from God Himself.

The Laws of Stewardship are rooted in the immovable ground of God's promises. They are sure and certain, truths that we can count on. They are the absolutely positive teachings of Jesus, such as the Law of Guaranteed Return that He stated like this: "Give, and it will be given to you," He said, "a good measure, pressed down, shaken together and running over, will be poured into your lap. For with the measure you use, it will be measured to you."[1] This is a principle that transcends time and place and circumstances. It is always true. If you give, it will be given to you. And not just an equal exchange. The return will be overflowing, super-abundant, bigger and better.

The purpose behind this promise is that we be motivated to give because it's a sensible investment. Spiritually speaking, there's virtually no risk but all reward. Better than a bond that's backed up by the full faith and credit of the United States Government, any gift given for God's glory is backed by the infinite resources of the Bank of Heaven. Whether the gift is money or some other form of contribution, God keeps perfect records. His promise is backed by His Word, and it's truly worth the Book it's written in. Give in His name and you will be blessed accordingly. There is no doubt about it, no cause for concern, no conditions under which the return is held back or held up.

LIVING THE LAWS

Here are some tips for putting God's promise into practice:

Check your eternal investment portfolio on a daily basis. In a financial portfolio there are investments that pay off and others that don't. Not so with spiritual investments, for they all pay a handsome return. The wise Christian comes to understand that these eternal investments are more important than temporal ones. The essence of this mindset is found in Jesus' words from the Sermon on the Mount: "Seek first the Kingdom of God and his righteousness, and all these things [the essentials of life] shall be added unto you."[2]

Don't allow worry to control your thoughts. Immediately before and immediately after His words about seeking first the Kingdom of God, Jesus addressed the problem of worry: "So do not worry, saying, 'What shall we eat?' or 'What shall we drink?' or 'What shall we wear?' For the pagans run after all these things, and your heavenly Father knows that you need them." Then He concludes, "Therefore do not worry about tomorrow, for tomorrow will worry about itself. Each day has enough trouble of its own."[3] The bottom line is clear: Banish worry from your mind and keep it out of your heart.

Don't give in order to get. Instead, give in order to bless, and you'll be blessed in return. That's a promise.

Scripture References:
[1] Luke 6:38
[2] Matthew 6:33
[3] Matthew 6:32, 34

5

THE LAW OF HILARIOUS GENEROSITY

God loves givers who give with the right attitude.

The scene was really nothing to laugh about, but it unleashed howls of delight, caused several fender-benders and brought traffic to a screeching halt on a busy freeway. People were literally jumping from their cars and rushing to grab the loot — several hundred thousand dollars worth — that was flying out the back door of an armored truck. The driver had failed to lock the door and the money was sucked out as if being removed by a giant vacuum. Even after the police arrived it took quite a while for order to be restored, and much of the money was never recovered.

The security guard failed to be diligent, and it cost him his job. Chances are he never imagined so many strangers would take advantage of his foolish misfortune. His experience reminds us that there are several forms of generosity. In the case of the flying funds, the generosity was completely unintentional. Sometimes, generosity is reluctant, particularly when one feels pressured to give. Generosity can also be manipulative, especially in situations where a gift is given for some ulterior motive. And it's not uncommon for generosity to be self-serving when one gives to gain some attention or advantage. In stark contrast, biblical generosity is like none of these. It is intentional, not the least bit reluctant, not manipulative and definitely not self-serving. Above all, it is full of joy. As the Apostle Paul explained, it is prompted by what one "has decided in his heart to give, not reluctantly or under compulsion, for God loves a cheerful giver."[1]

> Living by the Law of Hilarious Generosity, one does not give under the whiplash of necessity, complaining inwardly or being bitter in any way. Rather, one is thankful to even be able to give.

Herein is one of the most important principles for balanced Christian living, the Law of Hilarious Generosity. The word translated as "cheerful" in most English Bibles literally means "hilarious." It carries the idea of one who is uproariously delighted to give. Not grudgingly, like some sort of scrooge or miser, but freely and openly and happily. It's the absolute opposite of one who gives to God because he feels he can't refuse to give, or because someone else is giving and it would reflect poorly on him if he didn't give. Living by the Law of Hilarious Generosity, one does not give under the whiplash of necessity, complaining inwardly or being bitter in any way. Rather, one is thankful to even be able to give.

The hilarious giver remembers that Christ was infinitely rich yet for our sake became poor, laying aside the glory He had with the Father. With such an example of selfless giving, why would one not give cheerfully in return? God loves a cheerful giver because it is the right and honorable response to the greatness of His own giving. How could God feel in any way drawn toward a Christian who is willing that Heaven be bankrupted on his behalf then give as little as possible in return? The answer is, He isn't drawn to such a person.

Think of all the reasons to give with hilarious generosity: God, with a heart full of perfect love and compassion, gave His only Son to purchase our salvation. He gave the Holy Spirit as our eternal comforter, guide and teacher. He gave us the promise of life abundant here and life forever with Him in Heaven. He gave free access into His presence, allowing us to come with our petitions, and promising to hear and answer when we pray. He gave all this and so much more! How can we not give?

LIVING THE LAWS

When one gives with hilarious generosity, there is a conscious recognition of being a channel of blessings. We are passing on what He has passed to us. Imagine the feelings of the disciples when Jesus took those five loaves of bread and two fish and turned them into a feast for thousands. Think of the hilarious joy they felt handing out food to the hungry, seeing God multiply it as long as they kept sharing.[2] What a beautiful picture of what it's like for us when we give from the endless resources He entrusts to us.

God does not promise to solve all our problems, but He does promise to supply all our needs. The Bible assures us that "God will meet all your needs according to his glorious riches in Christ Jesus."[3] And, with our needs met, what more can we ask, and what more can we do than to give in return. He is "able to make all grace abound to you, so that in all things at all times, having all that you need, you will abound in every good work."[4] His purpose is that we serve Him fully and that we give hilariously in the process.

Keep in mind these practical perspectives for hilarious givers:

Don't talk yourself out of giving. Whenever you have a good opportunity to give, take it. In fact, look for opportunities to give generously, and live with an eager anticipation of how God will use you to bless others and please Him.

Take money seriously, but not too seriously. As Proverbs cautions, "Don't wear yourself out to get rich."[5] Money is important, but it isn't everything, and it can't bring true satisfaction. If you take money too seriously it can cloud your judgment and alter your motives. Accordingly, the generous giver remembers that money is a means to an end, not the end itself.

Give with a smile, not a cringe. When one gives with hilarious generosity, it's only natural to smile. After all, God's desire is not that we go through life simply collecting things and holding on to them. Instead, He wants us to give and give and give, just as He Himself does.

Scripture References:
[1] 2 Corinthians 9:7
[2] Mark 6:32-44
[3] Philippians 4:19
[4] 2 Corinthians 9:8
[5] Proverbs 23:4

6

THE LAW OF FAITHFUL DEPENDABILITY

Trustworthiness marks the true steward.

Bob the Bible college student was taking a test. After cruising through a number of questions on the life of the Apostle Paul he came upon one that stopped him like a brick wall. "In 150 to 200 words, describe Paul's attitude toward Epaphroditus." Being the quick thinker that he was, Bob reasoned that Epaphroditus was the "thorn in the flesh" from which Paul suffered. And, because he knew how that physical problem had been so debilitating to Paul, Bob wrote an appropriately lengthy explanation!

As Bob later learned to his chagrin, Epaphroditus was not a dreaded disease, but a dedicated disciple of Jesus Christ. In Paul's letter to the Philippians, he writes about this remarkable man, and the description is both encouraging and convicting. Epaphroditus was above all a Christian who could be counted on. In any situation at any time, Paul knew that Epaphroditus would be true and reliable. Many of his so-called friends and co-workers had deserted Paul, but not Epaphroditus. He was a living example of the Law of Faithful

Dependability that Paul taught to the Corinthians: "Now it is required that those who have been given a trust must prove faithful."[1] Another translation puts it this way: "Now what we look for in stewards is that they should be trustworthy."

Trustworthiness — faithful dependability — is the mark of the excellent steward. Epaphroditus epitomized this quality in all of his service for the Lord. In Philippians 2:25 he is described as a faithful worker, a faithful soldier and a faithful messenger. So deep was his commitment that he almost died for the work of Christ, risking his life to make up for the help the Philippians were unable to give to Paul. Epaphroditus understood perfectly that as stewards for Christ's sake we are co-workers, not competitors.

Christ-centered stewardship is the by-product of a Christ-like attitude. As Jesus explained to His disciples, "You know that those who are regarded as rulers of the Gentiles lord it over them, and their high officials exercise authority over them. Not so with you. Instead, whoever wants to become great among you must be your servant, and whoever wants to be first must be slave of all. For even the Son of Man did not come to be served, but to serve, and to give his life as a ransom for many."[2] At the most basic level, the true steward is a true servant.

Faithful dependability as a Christian steward relates to the management of money, but also to a great deal more. The "portfolio" for which we are responsible includes a wide range of components, and God's expectation is that we make the most of each one. Think of all the "assets" you have under management: your money, your time, your possessions, your opportunities, your influence, your relationships and much more. And to this long list can be added the spiritual assets with which we are entrusted: the Gospel of Christ, the mystery of godliness, the secret things of God. This is no small responsibility we bear, and to handle it rightly demands absolute faithfulness.

LIVING THE LAWS

In just about every one of Paul's epistles there is a clear statement about the priority of faithfulness. In the very first verse of Ephesians, he addresses "the saints in Ephesus, the *faithful* in Christ Jesus."[3] At the outset of Colossians, he writes, "To the holy and *faithful* brothers in Christ at Colosse."[4] To his spiritual son, Timothy, he repeatedly reinforced this same truth. And throughout the Bible we see that faithfulness is essential to serving God, to declaring His Word, to helping other believers and to handling situations of responsibility. From the Old Testament straight through the New, the wise, effective steward is shown to be utterly faithful. We see this virtue in Joseph when he was unjustly imprisoned. We observe it in Moses as he managed an entire nation in the middle of a wasteland. We find it in Daniel, who ran a government and could not be put down by his enemies, for "they could find no corruption in him, because he was trustworthy."[5] We see it in men like Epaphras whom Paul called "our dear fellow servant, who is a *faithful* minister of Christ."[6]

To be a trustworthy steward, you must handle the small things with the same regard as the big things. The Law of Faithful Dependability applies to the minor as well as the major things of life. Jesus said, "Whoever can be trusted with very little can also be trusted with much, and whoever is dishonest with very little will also be dishonest with much. So if you have not been trustworthy in handling worldly wealth, who will trust you with true riches? And if you have not been trustworthy with someone else's property, who will give you property of your own?"[7] The word is clear: the greater your dependability, the greater your blessing.

To be a trustworthy steward, you must see everything in life as sacred. For the believer, everything in life *is* sacred, and everything is to be devoted to the Lord. Whatever your talents, whatever your treasures, all are to be dedicated to God's purpose. "Whatever you do, do it all for the glory of God."[8]

Don't keep the secret things of God; share them liberally. As a Christian, you are given access to what the Bible calls mysterious truth; but you're also given permission to share the secret. Tell it freely and eagerly, for no area of faithful dependability is more important than the stewardship of the Gospel.

Scripture References:
[1] 1 Corinthians 4:2
[2] Mark 10:42-45
[3] Ephesians 1:1
[4] Colossians 1:2
[5] Daniel 6:4
[6] Colossians 1:7
[7] Luke 16:10-12
[8] 1 Corinthians 10:31

7

THE LAW OF
PARADOXICAL PARTICIPATION
*The richest generosity often comes
out of the deepest poverty.*

People are frequently confused about the difference between a paradox and an oxymoron. Both involve words which seem contradictory or incongruous. In the case of oxymorons, they're so interesting that "experts" faithfully record them. There's even a list of the Top 10 Oxymorons posted on several websites:

1. Government Organization
2. Same Difference
3. Taped Live
4. Plastic Glasses
5. Peace Force
6. Pretty Ugly
7. Head Butt
8. Working Vacation
9. Jumbo Shrimp
10. Tax Return

Oxymorons are intriguing and often downright funny, but they are different from paradoxes. The main distinction is that a paradox, although it may appear opposed to common sense, is nevertheless true. The Christian life is full of paradoxes, and the teaching of Jesus was replete with them. For example, He taught that...

To find you must lose[1]
To be rich you must be poor[2]
To live you must die[3]
To be first you must be last[4]
To be honored you must be humbled[5]

And to this list we could add others. Suffice it to say that paradoxes were a major component of Jesus's teaching, as they were in the writings of the Apostle Paul. One important example is found in Paul's description of the Macedonian believers: "Out of the most severe trial, their overflowing joy and their extreme poverty welled up in rich generosity."[6] These exemplary Christians personified the Law of Paradoxical Participation, the spiritual principle which tells us that *the richest generosity often comes out of the deepest poverty.*

True generosity is not measured by the size of the gift but by the spirit of the giver, and the Macedonians had a joyous spirit which transcended their severe circumstances. They were a living paradox: poor yet rich, pressed down yet rising up, humbled yet exalted. What a beautiful picture they were of the way believers should be. Their stewardship was exceptional, and it made an impact on others over a wide region.

The Law of Paradoxical Participation reminds us that God uses the simple things to confound the wise, and the little things to accomplish great deeds. He is not impressed with outward appearances or natural abilities because "the Lord looks upon the heart."[7] Some of the most effective servants of Jesus Christ have been the most unlikely men and women, people whose deepest longing was not be known, but to make Him known. "Little is much if God is in it," says the well-known song, and it's true.

John Wesley was a paradox, the most unlikely leader of a major religious movement. A mere five feet four inches tall, he never weighed more than 120 pounds. As a child he was often sickly and at age six he nearly died when his home caught fire. But in his 88 years of life, spanning nearly the entire 18th century, he travelled more than a quarter million miles on horseback, preaching the Word and establishing churches. Along the way he delivered over 42,000 sermons and authored more than 200 books. He felt limited and inadequate, but he always found encouragement in God's promise: "I can do everything through him who gives me strength."[8] As a steward he was so efficient that upon his death, after his debts were paid, he left an estate of less than ten pounds! He had given away nearly everything he ever acquired, not wanting to hoard or hang onto anything. What a testimony of godly diligence, and what a motivation to live by the Law of Paradoxical Participation.

LIVING THE LAWS

How shall we live by this important spiritual law? It comes down to several priorities:

Respond to need, not to pressure. The generous giver is prompted to give by seeing a need and being touched by it. There may be an emotional element, but the primary motive is spiritual in nature. Giving is never to be done out of pressure or compulsion because it's a matter of grace, not law. We are to give because we want to give, love to give, and are grateful we can give.

Have an open heart and an open hand. Openness is willingness, and nothing pleases God more than a heart that willingly yields to Him and a hand that willingly gives to Him. If one claims to have an open heart but is not willing to have an open hand, something is amiss, for the two should be inseparable.

Be a river, not a reservoir. Believers are channels, not containers. God's love and grace are to flow through us, not be held in us. As stewards, our compelling desire must be to constantly give and give and give as the river of God's blessings courses through our lives.

Scripture References:
[1] Matthew 10:39
[2] Matthew 5:3
[3] Luke 17:33
[4] Matthew 19:30
[5] Matthew 23:12
[6] 2 Corinthians 8:2
[7] 1 Samuel 16:7
[8] Philippians 4:13

8

THE LAW OF
SUPERNATURAL SUPPLY
God enables the giver to give beyond the ability to give.

O swald J. Smith was one of the most influential
Christian leaders of the 20th century. For nearly 50
years he served as senior pastor of Toronto's famed People's
Church, considered by many to be the most missions-minded
congregation in North America. During Dr. Smith's eventful
tenure at the church it was not unusual for more than half the
annual income to be invested in missionary endeavors around
the globe. Oswald Smith did not shy away from the subject of
giving to the Lord's work; indeed, he spent much of his time
calling upon believers to contribute as generously, sacrificially
and energetically as possible. A prolific writer, he authored
numerous books and coined more than his share of memorable phrases. But undoubtedly the most enduring is a term
still widely used: the "Faith Promise Offering."

According to Pastor Smith, a Faith Promise Offering is a
commitment to give a specific amount to God's work based
upon God's future supply of the funds rather than one's present

ability to give the money. The essential idea is to make a specific promise by faith, relying upon the Lord to provide and enable fulfillment of the promise. As the reasoning goes, if God doesn't supply, you don't give, because it's up to Him to provide. And, as thousands upon thousands of testimonies confirm, God *will* supply and He *will* bless the one who puts faith in His ability. To Dr. Smith, this wasn't hocus-pocus or some kind of mysterious occurrence. It was simply God keeping His Word and providing for His children as they trusted in Him explicitly. Its basis is the Law of Supernatural Supply, the principle which teaches us that *God enables the believer to give beyond the ability to give.*

The Apostle Paul said of the Macedonian Christians that "they gave as much as they were able, and even beyond their ability."[1] They didn't call it a "Faith Promise Offering" but that's what it was because their confidence was firmly based upon God's power to provide. They were able to give beyond their ability because God has no limitations and they trusted Him as the great enabler. The lesson for us is that we can give beyond our ability to give only by choosing to rely upon God's supply rather than our own. Promising to give what one does not have may seem foolish, but only if it is not prompted by faith. If it is an act of faith, God will honor the trust placed in Him.

LIVING THE LAWS

Practical Christian living is not a natural thing. By this we don't mean that it's abnormal or odd, but that it transcends the natural world. At its core, it is supernatural. The power which God gives the believer is not natural power but supernatural power. The provision He makes is not natural but supernatural. This is an absolute law in the economy of stewardship, and it must not escape our attention.

Bid farewell to the scarcity mindset. Far too many Christians are more prone to think in terms of scarcity than abundance. They focus on what they don't have rather than thinking about what they could have through God's abundant provision. The promise of Jesus is unlimited: "I tell you the truth," He says, "I am the gate for the sheep. All who ever came before me were thieves and robbers, but the sheep did not listen to them. I am the gate; whoever enters through me will be saved. He will come in and go out, and find pasture. The thief comes only to steal and kill and destroy; I have come that they might have life, and have it to the full."[2] The King James version states the last verse, "I am come that they might have life and have it more abundantly." This is the truth which should overshadow all else, and our attitude must be energized by God's abundant assurance.

> Practical Christian living is not a natural thing. By this we don't mean that it's abnormal or odd, but that it transcends the natural world. At its core it is supernatural.

Base your promises upon God's promises. When you think about giving, and specifically when you make a commitment to give, don't focus on your limitations but on His limitlessness. Make promises by faith, remembering that "the just shall live by faith."[3] Put your confidence in the Lord, knowing that He longs to show Himself strong on behalf of all who trust in Him.

Extend the limits of your spiritual comfort zone. It isn't God's desire that we live easy, comfortable lives. After all, we are engaged in a battle — a spiritual conflict that will continue until God brings history to a climax. Don't be afraid of the warfare, and don't shy away from difficulty. Keep your focus on Jesus, the author and finisher of our faith. In every dimension of stewardship, think of Him above all else.

Scripture References:
[1] 2 Corinthians 8:3
[2] John 10:7-10
[3] Romans 1:17

9

THE LAW OF
EAGER WILLINGNESS

Wise stewards joyfully choose to
support God's work and do God's will.

The greatest power God has given to man is the power of choice. He did not create us as mindless beings programmed to behave in a certain way; rather, He gave us a free will with the ability to choose good or bad, right or wrong. Writing on this subject, C. S. Lewis observed: "God has made it a rule for Himself that He won't alter people's character by force. He can and will alter them — but only if the people will let Him. He would rather have a world of free beings, with all its risks, than a world of people who did right like machines because they couldn't do anything else. The more we succeed in imagining what a world of perfect automatic beings would be like, the more, I think, we shall see His wisdom."

In stewardship, choice is a never-ending concern, for we must constantly decide how to manage everything that God puts in our care. Most important of all is that we decide with true purpose, joyfully choosing to support God's work and do God's will. The ruling principle is the Law of Eager Willingness, the spiritual precept that tells us to respond with desire, openness and yielded hearts. Paul commended the Christians at Corinth for having this attitude: "You were the first not only to give but also to have the desire to do so. Now finish the work, so that your eager willingness to do it may be matched by your completion of it, according to your means." Then he concludes, "For if the willingness is there, the gift is acceptable according to what one has, not according to what he does not have."[1]

Eager willingness to give has always been a hallmark of dedicated believers. We see it in the Old Testament when God's people gave toward the building of the tabernacle and later for the construction of the temple. When King David led the effort to build the temple, he appealed for gifts because the project was immeasurably important. After all, the temple was to be the most impressive building ever — a "palatial structure not for man but for the Lord God."[2] The building materials were unlike anything we would use today — gold, silver, onyx, turquoise and precious stones. It would be more grand than anything else on earth, and it was deserving of special stewardship.

> Since everything we have and everything we are is the result of His grace, why not be eager? Why not be willing? Nothing else makes sense.

David set the example in his giving, dedicating all his kingly wealth and his personal treasures to this great project. Then, moved by his example, leaders at every other level began to give — leaders of families, officers of the tribes, commanders of thousands, commanders of hundreds. The Scripture says that they all "gave willingly"[3] toward the work.

And, when the offering was complete, "the people rejoiced at the willing response of their leaders, for they had given freely and wholeheartedly to the Lord."[4] King David then spoke for everyone when he praised God openly and said, "But who am I, and who are my people, that we should be able to give as generously as this? Everything comes from you, and we have given you only what comes from your hand."[5]

LIVING THE LAWS

Eager willingness to give is the most reasonable, intelligent response to God's blessings upon us. Since everything we have and everything we are is the result of His grace, why not be eager? Why not be willing? Nothing else makes sense.

The willing giver chooses to be open toward God and man. Too many believers are closed and exclusive when they ought to be open and inclusive. Openness is the normal state for a yielded heart. To be otherwise is to limit the flow of God's blessing. It's a daily choice, simply voicing one's yieldedness, saying "Lord, here am I, use me as your servant, guide me as your steward."

The willing giver encourages others to give, inspiring them by example. Of all the ways in which King David inspired his people as a leader, his generous giving had perhaps the most impact because it was something literally every one of his subjects could imitate. Not everyone could lead forces into battle, nor judge complex situations, nor oversee an entire nation's well being; but everyone could give generously, and they were inspired to do so by a powerful example. When you give willingly, God can use your example to encourage others to do likewise.

The willing giver sees the pleasure of sacrifice, not the pain. Giving often demands sacrifice, and sacrifice always has a measure of pain. But, ironically, sacrifice can also have its share of pleasure if we simply remember why we're doing what we do, why we're giving as we are. What is our sacrifice, really? Are we not just giving back to God what He gave to us in the first place? Willingness to give, whatever the cost, ought to be prompted by the pleasure of serving a gracious God.

Scripture References:
[1] 2 Corinthians 8:10-12
[2] 1 Chronicles 29:1
[3] 1 Chronicles 29:6
[4] 1 Chronicles 29:9
[5] 1 Chronicles 29:14

10

THE LAW OF
RECIPROCAL SUPPLY

Through meeting others' needs we meet our own.

T he church is described by many metaphors in Scripture:
It is called a flock[1], a vineyard[2], a temple[3], a family[4], a
building[5] and a bride.[6] But most directly and specifically it is
called a body.[7] As believers we are members of the body of
Christ. We belong to Him and to one another in the most
remarkable, most significant union. Like the members of a
physical body, we the members of Christ's spiritual body serve
a variety of purposes and fill a wide range of roles. As the Bible
says, "The body is a unit, though it is made up of many parts;
and though all its parts are many, they form one body. So it is
with Christ."[8]

As we relate to one another, there's no room for jeal-
ous comparison. "The eye cannot say to the hand, 'I don't
need you!' And the head cannot say to the feet, 'I don't need
you!' On the contrary, those parts of the body that seem to be
weaker are indispensable, and the parts that we think are less
honorable we treat with special honor."[9] This interconnected-
ness is a key element of biblical stewardship. It was the main

concern when Paul wrote to the Corinthians, "Our desire is not that others might be relieved while you are hard pressed, but that there might be equality. At the present time, your plenty will supply what they need, so that in turn their plenty will supply what you need."[10] He was stating a vital principle, the Law of Reciprocal Supply, which teaches us that *through meeting others' needs we meet our own.*

> Christian stewardship is not fulfilled in a vacuum. It is not merely an individual responsibility, for we belong to one another and must think of one another, not just ourselves.

From the earliest days of the Church, the Law of Reciprocal Supply was in effect. Acts chapter 2 describes how it worked among the first Christians: "All the believers were together and had everything in common. Selling their possessions and goods, they gave to anyone as he had need."[11] This was not communism but communion, the unfettered commitment of believers to one another, meeting needs and giving generously as they together met the challenges of each day. Each person was exercising his or her gifts for the greater benefit of the body. They were reciprocating, which according to *Webster's*, is "giving and taking mutually."

The importance of spiritual gifts must not be underestimated because without them we cannot function properly in Christ's body. A spiritual gift is a divinely ordained ability through which Christ enables His Church to accomplish its purposes on earth. In short, it is a Spirit-given capacity for Christian service. The source of each gift is God Himself, and the nature of each gift is purely spiritual. It is not a talent, for talents have to do with natural abilities. Talents instruct, inspire or entertain on a natural level; but spiritual gifts are for service, ministry and edification. Talents and gifts may be related, but they are not one and the same. For example, a person who is naturally visionary may be given the gift of faith. A natural teacher may be given the gift of teaching. These are merely possibilities; the actual giving of spiritual gifts is determined by God alone.

A. T. Pierson, founder of the Christian & Missionary Alliance, observed seven principles pertaining to spiritual gifts. We are wise to remember them:

1. Every believer has some gift, therefore all should be encouraged.
2. No one has all the gifts, therefore all should be humble.
3. All gifts are for the Body, therefore all should be harmonious.
4. All gifts are for the Lord, therefore all should be contented.
5. All gifts are mutually helpful, therefore all should be faithful.
6. All gifts promote the whole Body's health, therefore none can be dispensed with.
7. All gifts depend upon the Holy Spirit's empowerment, therefore none should be out of fellowship with Him.

LIVING THE LAWS

One fact that we keep coming back to is that Christian stewardship is not fulfilled in a vacuum. It is not merely an individual responsibility, for we belong to one another and must think of one another, not just ourselves. To live by the Law of Reciprocal Supply is to maintain an upward and outward attitude, not an inward focus. There's a memorable children's song that says it simply and brilliantly:

Jesus and Others and You,
what a wonderful way to spell JOY.
Jesus and Others and You,
in the life of each girl and each boy.
J is for Jesus, who died in our place;
O is for Others we know face to face;
Y is for You, and whatever you do,
Put yourself last to spell JOY.

This is how we experience true reciprocity, finding real joy through serving the Lord and caring for others as faithful stewards.

When you face a big need, try to find someone else with that same need. Pray for them, help them, and do everything in your ability to meet their need. Focus your interest and care on others, and rely upon the Lord to meet your needs and bless your service. Put the principle of reciprocity to work and see what God will do.

Use your gifts. Giving monetary gifts is important and needful, but giving ministry gifts in service for Christ is vital. Know your giftedness and use it for God's glory.

Look constantly for Body-building opportunities. Of course, we're referring to building up the spiritual body, the Body of Christ; and the way this happens is through ministry to one another. We are to forbear one another[12], forgive one another[13], submit to one another[14], admonish one another[15], comfort one another[16] and exhort one another.[17] By doing these things, we grow spiritually stronger and healthier.

Scripture References:
[1] John 10:1-15, 26-30
[2] John 15:1-10
[3] Romans 14:17
[4] Ephesians 2:19
[5] Ephesians 2:20-22
[6] Ephesians 5:22-32
[7] 1 Corinthians 12:12-27
[8] 1 Corinthians 12:12
[9] 1 Corinthians 12:21-23
[10] 2 Corinthians 8:13-14
[11] Acts 2:44-45
[12] Ephesians 4:2
[13] Colossians 3:13
[14] Ephesians 5:21
[15] Colossians 3:16
[16] 1 Thessalonians 4:18
[17] Hebrews 3:13

11

THE LAW OF CONSTRUCTIVE CONTRIBUTION

The work of God is to be done by the people of God giving according to the will of God.

John Wesley was once approached by one of his parishioners, an earnest man who felt his service was unimportant. "If only I could preach like you, Mr. Wesley," he said, "I would be so happy and fulfilled." Wesley replied, "Sir, we are building God's temple. Go now and read the third chapter of Nehemiah and learn that he who repaired the dung gate was counted of as much honor as he who worked on the gate of the fountain. All did their bit; you and I can do no more."

Wesley understood very well one of the most important tenets of stewardship, the Law of Constructive Contribution. This is a principle which tells us that *the work of God is to be done by the people of God giving according to the will of God.* We find examples of this principle in practice throughout the Bible, but perhaps the most memorable is the story of Nehemiah and the project to rebuild the wall around Jerusalem. The lessons of that experience are profoundly instructive to anyone who wants to do the work of God according to the will of God.

Nehemiah was a trusted aide and advisor to King Artaxerxes I of Persia. While serving in the palace one day, he received a visit from his brother, Hanani, who brought news from Jerusalem. The report was not good: Hanani told him, "Those who survived the exile and are back in the province are in great trouble and disgrace. The wall of Jerusalem is broken down, and its gates have been burned with fire."[1] As an exiled Jew himself, Nehemiah was overwhelmed with the bad news.

> The criticism was prompted by progress, which often occurs when God's people start to make things happen.

He sat down and wept, mourning and fasting and praying for several days. Then, with bold initiative, he asked for permission to go to Jerusalem to lead the effort to rebuild the wall. The king gave him his full blessing, plus access to vast resources of timber for the project. He even provided for Nehemiah to be accompanied by army officers and cavalry on the long journey. Upon arriving in Jerusalem, Nehemiah assessed the damage, determined his plan and then rallied the people. "Come," he told them, "let us rebuild the wall of Jerusalem, and we will no longer be in disgrace." The people were stirred by his words and replied, "Let us start rebuilding!"[2] And so the work began.

As God's people came together to do God's work according to God's will, they committed their resources, their time and their energies to the task. And there was no shortage of challenges, for God's will did not allow for the wall to be rebuilt without a struggle. Before the job was even half-done, the workers were bombarded with sarcasm and criticism. One loathsome opponent, a government official named Sanballat, "became angry and was greatly incensed. He ridiculed the Jews, and in the presence of his associates and the army of Samaria, he said, 'What are those feeble Jews doing? Will they restore their wall? Will they offer their sacrifices? Will they finish in a day? Can they bring the stones back to life from those heaps of rubble — burned as they are?'" And, as if his attacks weren't enough, another enemy, Tobiah, said, "What they are building — if even a fox climbed up on it, he would break down their wall of stones!"[3]

The criticism was prompted by progress, which often occurs when God's people start to make things happen. The devotion and determination of this small band of Jews ought to have evoked admiration, but it wasn't to be. The opponents simply couldn't bear to see anything positive happening. To them, any change in the status quo was a threat; and, even though Sanballat and Tobiah weren't the best of friends, they were drawn together by mutual hatred of God's servants. Critics usually run with critics; and while not all criticism is of the devil, this certainly was.

In the pursuit of constructive contribution, the problems were numerous: Anger. Ridicule. Questioning. Criticism. Sarcasm. Treachery. Threats. The enemies called the rebuilding project the Jews' wall, when in fact it was God's wall. In reality, they were criticizing God. Nehemiah recognized this, and he took decisive action to counteract the opposition. First, he prayed. "Hear us, O our God, for we are despised. Turn their insults back on their own heads. Give them over as plunder in a land of captivity."[4] Nehemiah's prayer seems severe until we remember that God had already pronounced judgment on the enemies of Israel. Nehemiah was simply asking God to fulfill that judgment. The battle against God's foes would be waged first of all in prayer. Nehemiah didn't throw punches; he prayed. He resisted the temptation to strike back, because he knew that God was in control. He and the people persisted against the tide of opposition. "So we rebuilt the wall till all of it reached half its height, for the people worked with all their heart."[5]

LIVING THE LAWS

The Law of Constructive Contribution was ruling in their hearts, and they kept going in spite of all that stood in the way. In just 52 days, the wall was rebuilt and the people celebrated God's blessing and empowerment. If we look closely at their experience, the lessons are clearly applicable to us as stewards today:

Intensify your persistence in prayer. The waves of persecution never let up while the rebuilding went on, but God's people had a stronger weapon: "We prayed to our God and posted a guard day and night to meet this threat."[6] Exercising common sense, they set up a defense. They did what was necessary to complement their prayers. If you want to counteract your home being burglarized, don't just pray, put in an alarm system.

Expect difficulty when you do what's right. Great opportunity is often accompanied by great opposition. The Apostle Paul said of the work in Ephesus, "A great door for effective ministry has opened to me, and there are many who oppose me."[7] He chose to think primarily about the great open door, not the daunting opponents. The easiest thing to do when confronted by difficulty is to give up, and nothing pleases Satan or the critics more than for the negative to cancel or neutralize the positive. It's crucial to keep going, no matter what is in the way, no matter what threatens to prevent you from doing God's will.

Don't give up or give in. Nehemiah and the workers were invincible because they were in the very center of God's will. They would not give up or give in. Faced with deceit, distraction and discouragement on all sides, they kept relying on God's power and He gave them the victory. God's promise to us is no different from the one those believers carried in their hearts. John's first epistle reminds us: "You, dear children, are from God and have overcome them, because the one who is in you is greater than the one who is in the world."[8]

Scripture References:
[1] Nehemiah 1:3
[2] Nehemiah 2:17, 18
[3] Nehemiah 4:1-3
[4] Nehemiah 4:4
[5] Nehemiah 4:6
[6] Nehemiah 4:9
[7] 1 Corinthians 16:9
[8] 1 John 4:4

12

THE LAW OF
PURPOSEFUL BLESSING
We are made rich in every way
to be generous on every occasion.

The year was 1903. Theodore Roosevelt ruled with a
strong hand as President of the United States. Master
engineers had launched a massive project to link the oceans by
digging a great canal through the Isthmus of Panama. Henry
Ford was tinkering with his newest invention, the Model T
automobile. Two brothers from Ohio, Orville and Wilbur
Wright, had just achieved the first successful flight of an air-
plane. It was an era of innovation, an age of breathtaking
advancement. The future was brimming with promise, especially for William Borden, a bright young high school gradu-
ate from Chicago.

William was an unusual teenager, most notably because
he was a millionaire. As heir to the Borden Dairy fortune, life
was rich with possibilities and the world was his to discover. In
fact, that is literally what young Bill did after his graduation —
he discovered the world, travelling around the globe for an
entire year. He encountered foreign cultures and explored
intriguing places; and everywhere he went he was touched by

the desperate needs of people. In a letter to his parents he announced his intentions to devote his life to missionary service. In effect, he had decided to give up all the pleasures of his position, all the advantages at his disposal. In his Bible he wrote two words: No Reserves.

In the fall of 1905, William Borden enrolled at Yale University. One of his classmates later wrote of him, "He came to college far ahead spiritually of any of us. We who were his classmates learned to lean on him and find in him a strength that was solid as a rock, just because of his settled purpose and consecration." At Yale, Borden was not only an exceptional student but a gifted leader, personally spearheading a movement of spiritual renewal on the campus. So powerful was the movement that, by his senior year, over 1,000 of Yale's 1,300 students were attending weekly Bible fellowships. Off campus, Borden was active as well, rescuing down-and-outers and drunks from the streets of New Haven. He established the Yale Hope Mission to give them a place of refuge and rehabilitation.

Upon his graduation from Yale, William could have moved directly into the huge family business or taken any of numerous job offers. But his intentions to become a missionary never wavered. For him, there remained only one more stage of preparation, a course of theological studies at Princeton Seminary, which he completed in two years. After receiving his degree, William was ready to take the boldest step of all, a one-way trip to Egypt. There he would learn Arabic in order to reach Muslims with the Gospel. Leaving family and fortune behind, he set sail across the Atlantic. On the way, he wrote two more words in his Bible: No Retreats.

William arrived in Cairo full of anticipation and ready for the challenge. With customary zeal he immersed himself in the task at hand; but within days he became very weak. He had been stricken with spinal meningitis, and it was a force he could not withstand. A short time later, William Whiting Borden died at the age of 25.

When the news of William's death was cabled from Egypt, tears flowed and hearts ached an ocean away. One biographer wrote, "It seemed as though a wave of sorrow went round the world...for William Borden not only gave his wealth, but himself, in a way so joyous and natural that it was manifestly a privilege rather than a sacrifice." In terms of human logic, the death of such a promising young man was a waste. But that was not William's perspective. During the last fleeting days of his life, in labored handwriting, he had penned two more words in his Bible: No Regrets.

The legacy of William Borden can be summed up in those six poignant words he recorded so deliberately: No Reserves. No Retreats. No Regrets. He had taken to heart the incontrovertible truths of biblical stewardship which were written down by another missionary, the Apostle Paul, many centuries before. One of those truths is the Law of Purposeful Blessing, which Paul expressed in his second letter to the believers in Corinth: "Now he who supplies seed to the sower and bread for food will also supply and increase your store of seed and will enlarge the harvest of your righteousness. You will be made rich in every way so that you can be generous on every occasion."[1] Examine these words closely and you'll see a promise coupled with a purpose. The promise — "You will be made rich in every way" — is an assurance of abundant giving, the certainty that God will provide you with everything you need. The purpose — "So that you can be generous on every occasion" — is an encouragement to abundant generosity, cheerfully and willingly giving to others in response to God's gifts to you.

William Borden, though just a young man, had learned well the Law of Purposeful Blessing. He took full advantage of every way in which he had been made rich in order to show generosity to others at every opportunity. Everything in his life — indeed, life itself — he had dedicated to the Savior. William Borden did not live a long life, but he lived a full life — full of hope, full of grace, full of faith and full of love for God and others.

> The legacy of William Borden can be summed up in those six poignant words he recorded so deliberately:
> No Reserves.
> No Retreats.
> No Regrets.
> He had taken to heart the incontrovertible truths of biblical stewardship.

LIVING THE LAWS

Giving on purpose begins with living on purpose. The purpose of your life should be the basis and motivating force behind your giving. If your life purpose is to honor God and serve Him wholeheartedly, everything you give — whether it is money, time, energy, influence or some other gift — is to be an expression of that foundational purpose. There should be no conflict between why you live and why you give: they are part and parcel of a Christ-centered continuum. If any other motivations worm their way into your heart, and if you give in to those motivations, you will lose the joy and the blessing. When you write a check to your church, for example, don't think about the benefits of tax deductibility; think about God's blessings which enable you both to live and to give.

Blessing others generously is a delight, not a duty. Many Christians trudge through life burdened down by an inordinate sense of duty. They've been taught that God demands full obedience and compliance with His laws, which is absolutely true; but they've been taught in a way that binds rather than frees. They are instilled with a view of God that leaves them emotionally restricted instead of spiritually free. Christian obedience is not an oppressive, burdensome thing. It is the joyous response of a grateful heart. Likewise, Christian generosity is the natural expression of one who purposefully blesses others. It is a delight, not a duty.

Stewardship is measured qualitatively, not just quantitatively. Some would argue that William Borden could have been a more effective steward if he had used his great wealth to underwrite Christian ministry. They would question whether it was really logical for him to take such a rough path when a smooth road was so readily available. However, what matters most to God is not our logic but our love — the love that denies self, takes up the cross and follows Him unreservedly. This is what Jesus was talking about when he told a rich young man of the ruling class to sell everything he had and give it all to the poor. Unfortunately, the young man was not willing to take such a drastic step because he loved his possessions more than he loved God. Christian stewardship is first and foremost a qualitative matter of the heart, not a quantitative measurement of one's gifts.

Scripture Reference:
[1] 2 Corinthians 9:11

13

THE LAW OF
CONSISTENT COLLECTION
Consistent giving facilitates consistent ministry.

The impoverished Christians at Jerusalem were in dire straits. We don't know precisely why they were suffering so severely, but their situation was compellingly bad — so bad that the Apostle Paul instructed the believers in other places to take up a special offering for them. Paul reasoned that "if the Gentiles have shared in the Jews' spiritual blessings, they owe it to the Jews to share with them their material blessings."[1] But it was important that the offering be given in the right spirit and in the right way. They were to set aside an amount of money the first day of every week, in proportion to the Lord's blessing upon them during the week.

"Now about the collection for God's people: Do what I told the Galatian churches to do. On the first day of every week, each one of you should set aside a sum of money in keeping with his income, saving it up, so that when I come no collections will have to be made. Then, when I arrive, I will give letters of introduction to the men you approve and send them with your gift to Jerusalem."[2]

In the King James Version, a key phrase in this passage reads, "as the Lord had prospered..." The word "prospered" has a wonderful meaning in the original Greek language of the New Testament. Literally, it means "blessing in the good way." That "good way" might be a good way in business; it might be a good way in relationships; it might be a good way in deeper fellowship with God. And, while the essential idea is to give of our material wealth as God enables us to obtain it, there is also a prosperity of the soul that He gives. It is inadequate to measure our prosperity only in dollars and cents when He gives us so much in divine love, grace and mercy. We would be wise to think in terms of giving to God according to the full measure of His blessing. Imagine, for example, that each time He unfolded a new truth to you or answered a prayer or delivered you from danger, you would honor His gifts with an appropriate response. Imagine how much richer your life would be. In this larger context, financial gifts seem the very least we can do in obedience to the Lord and appreciation for His goodness.

> While the essential idea is to give of our material wealth as God enables us to obtain it, there is also a prosperity of the soul that He gives. It is inadequate to measure our prosperity only in dollars and cents when He gives us so much in divine love, grace and mercy.

The Law of Consistent Collection, the principle at the core of Paul's instruction in these verses, teaches us that *consistent giving facilitates consistent ministry.* There isn't a legalistic demand that we give an amount of money every week to the Lord's work, but that we give regularly and consistently. God's desire is that things be done decently and in order, not in chaos or uncertainty. When there is a need, His plan is that His people give responsively to meet it. The ongoing operation of a church's ministry, for example, requires the ongoing support of faithful believers. A majority of Christian leaders believe that the foundation of God's plan for giving is the tithe — ten percent of one's income. Since ancient times, the tithe has been a standard (perhaps a minimum standard) for what one gives gratefully to God. In the first tithe described in the Bible, Abraham gave Melchizedek the high priest a tenth of everything he had. It was an expression of gratitude to God for victory and to God's priest for the sanctuary he had provided.[3]

LIVING THE LAWS

Consistent contributions to the Lord's work are acts of worship, expressions of devotion to Him. It is important that we give on a continuing basis because it demonstrates that we recognize the Lordship of Christ. The spirit in which we give is also important:

Give with consistent gratitude. Everything in our hands has come from His hand, and we are but channels through which God's work is carried out. When we live in primary consideration of Him, gratitude minimizes our tendencies to squander our resources on self-gratification.

Give with consistent sacrifice. David said, "I will not sacrifice to the Lord my God burnt offerings that cost me nothing"[4] Sacrifice always involves cost, but it has less to do with how much one gives than how much one gives up. In the measure of sacrifice, we must ask, what does this truly cost me? When we pay a sacrificial price we accentuate the sacred over the secular.

Give with consistent praise. The distinction between gratitude and praise is this: gratitude is appreciation for what God has done, praise is appreciation for who God is. King David knew the distinction: "Now our God, we give you thanks and praise your glorious name."[5] As you worship the Lord daily in times of meditation and prayer, remember that He is your provider and commit yourself consistently to being a good steward of His provision.

Scripture References:
[1] Romans 15:27
[2] 1 Corinthians 16:1-3
[3] Genesis 14:20
[4] 2 Samuel 24:24
[5] 1 Chronicles 29:13

14

THE LAW OF PROPORTIONATE PARTICIPATION

God's provision dictates the believer's proportion.

T he images are painfully familiar: hollow-cheeked mothers, their faces etched with despair, children with distended stomachs, desperate people dying of malnutrition. Whenever we see such dreadful sights, we feel a stirring of compassion for those who suffer and we long to help in some way. At the same time, we're reminded that dire circumstances have plagued mankind throughout history. Jesus said that the poor would be with us always, and He declared that the priority, regardless of one's lot in life, is to glorify God and trust Him explicitly. Whatever the situation, whatever the limitations, we are to worship and serve the Lord wholeheartedly. Just as Jesus loved without limits and gave without restriction, so are we to love and give in proportion to His provision for us.

Genuine worship is characterized by genuine faith, and sometimes that faith must be proven in the face of extreme conditions. Let's take a look at two examples, one from Old Testament days and the other from the New Testament era.

In 1 Kings 17 we read of a certain widow from the region called Zarephath. Not only was she without a husband, she was also without any observable resources except a few ounces of oil and a handful of flour. The circumstances were severe because a three-year drought had devastated Israel, due to the people's disobedience to God. Elijah the prophet, trusting in God to provide his daily bread, was instructed by the Lord to go to the widow for his supply. When he arrived, she was gathering sticks to build the fire for her final supper, since she had enough for only one more meal for herself and her son. She was resigned to starve to death.

Elijah asked the widow for water, then for a piece of bread. She then explained her circumstances, and Elijah did what seems to be irrational and even ridiculous to the natural mind. He told her to not fear, but to make him a small cake, and then make one for her son. Then he promised her that she would have sufficient supply until the rains were restored.

She obeyed, and God fulfilled His word. Facing death, both Elijah and the widow were responding to specific instructions from the Lord, not wild suppositions. For him to make such a request would take great faith. For her to simply respond demonstrated an authentic, sacrificial act of worship. When she engaged with God according to His terms and in the way He established, God's work continued and her needs were amply and miraculously provided for. By an act of her will she took the leap of faith and gave what she was trusting in to sustain her life, if even for just a little while.[1]

The essential purpose of this story is to remind us that giving is an integral act of worship. The widow gave something out of her own need. She gave first to sustain the work of the Lord and fulfill the word of the Lord. God then opened

his windows of grace and miraculously multiplied her gift —
and the divine supply came for at least one full year.

Now let's turn our attention to a group of believers
who lived several centuries later in the region of Macedonia.
As we've already seen in previous chapters, Paul says some
interesting things about these brothers and sisters in Christ.
He wrote to the Corinthians: "And now, brothers, we want
you to know about the grace that God has given the
Macedonian churches. Out of the most severe trial, their overflowing joy and their extreme poverty welled up in rich generosity. For I testify that they gave as much as they were able,
and even beyond their ability. Entirely on their own, they
urgently pleaded with us for the privilege of sharing in this service to the saints. And they did not do as we expected, but
they gave themselves first to the Lord and then to us in keeping with God's will."[2]

The young churches of Macedonia were persecuted
severely and were materially poor, yet spiritually they lived
above the extreme conditions and excelled in giving it their all.
Specifically, they gave to a ministry project that the Apostle
Paul had initiated; and they gave in a most remarkable way:
sacrificially, beyond their ability, willingly and eagerly — of
themselves to God and of their resources to God's work.

The Law of Proportionate Provision — a powerful
principle of stewardship — is evident both in the widow of
Zarephath and the Christians of Macedonia. This law teaches
us that *God's provision dictates the believer's proportion.* In
other words, what He provides determines what we give. If
He gives a little, from that little we are to give; if He gives
abundantly, from that abundance we are to give. Whatever He
provides, regardless of the depth or breadth, determines the

measure of our giving. As Jesus reminded His disciples, "To whom much is given, much is required."[3]

LIVING THE LAWS

Don't worry about what you have or don't have to give. The Law of Proportionate Provision is a reassuring truth of Scripture because it eliminates the pressure of thinking about what we have or don't have to give. Relying upon the Lord and depending upon Him as our source, we grow in grace as we give. In the process, giving becomes a therapeutic experience, for as we die to self we come alive in faith.

Give in proportion to everything you have received. Proportionate participation in the work of God involves much more than money. Whatever God has given you, in whatever measure, is to be dedicated to him. Your talents, your abilities, your material wealth, your time — all are resources from which you can give.

Deny the dominance of worldly thinking. Worldly attitudes emphasize *me* and *mine*, and they can suck us into a whirlpool of obsessions. John the Apostle cautioned, "Do not love the world or anything in the world. If anyone loves the world, the love of the Father is not in him."[4] As believers in Jesus Christ, we belong to a different universe. Our citizenship is in heaven, and if we act as if our citizenship is in this corrupt world, we lose sight and we lose the fullness of God's blessing.

God will provide. That's a certainty. And the proportion of His provision defines the proportion of our giving.

Scripture References:
[1] 1 Kings 17:2-24
[2] 2 Corinthians 8:1-5
[3] Luke 12:48
[4] 1 John 2:15

15

THE LAW OF PERSONAL INITIATIVE

Desire precedes duty in the grace of giving.

S everal years ago in the unlikely town of Fulton, Missouri, city officials requested that huge chunks of concrete be hauled onto the local college campus. In preparation for a major event, they wanted to build an appropriate backdrop. An historic speech was to be delivered in their little city, and the concrete slabs would be perfect for the occasion. They weren't much to look at; in fact, they were severely scarred and covered with graffiti. But in that setting on that day, they couldn't have been more beautiful.

The speech was to be given by Mikail Gorbachev, ex-premier of the once-powerful Soviet Union. His address would be delivered in the same place as one given nearly half a century earlier by Sir Winston Churchill. Speaking from the same podium, Churchill had coined the phrase "Iron Curtain" to describe the enslavement of Eastern Europe. Decades later, an ex-Soviet leader would stand on the same campus and speak about...freedom. Displayed prominently behind him would be those unsightly concrete pillars from the recently-fallen Berlin Wall — actual remnants of that once-daunting "Iron Curtain."

Freedom. What a wonderful word it is, and what a wonderful state to live in. Here in the United States, we are blessed with a measure of freedom that is remarkable in the annals of modern history. Yet this social freedom pales in comparison with the spiritual freedom that has been given to us in Jesus Christ. In Him, we have been liberated eternally. And because of the freedom He has given us, we are able to give wholeheartedly and unreservedly to Him. He allows us to exercise this freedom by our own determination. In the economy of Christian stewardship, this is the Law of Personal Initiative, the principle which underscores that *desire precedes duty in the grace of giving*. This was the principle at work in the Macedonians when they gave "entirely on their own."[1] They took the initiative in giving, exercising their freedom in an expression of true generosity.

"Freely you have received, freely give,"[2] said Jesus to His disciples when He sent them out to preach the Gospel of the Kingdom. He wanted them to be motivated by the fact that they had been given something very valuable, yet, paradoxically, were able to give it away and still keep it. They had been freely given the redemptive truth of Christ and, with His empowerment, they were mobilized to go forth and give it away to others. As their lives had been changed, others' lives would be changed by the same transformational truth.

Jesus doesn't force us to be His disciples. Never does he coerce anyone into His service. His invitation is free, His offer of eternal life is free, the indwelling of His Spirit is free, the opportunity to serve Him is free. He freely took the initiative in giving His life as the substitutionary payment for our sin. In obedience to the Father, He gave everything, setting aside His heavenly state to be robed in human flesh. He lived perfectly, died sacrificially, rose again triumphantly and ascended back to heaven gloriously. And He didn't charge us a thing, which is good because we couldn't pay the price anyway. However, what we can do is serve Him out of grateful hearts and loving devotion. He has given beyond all measure, all at His personal initiative. How can we not as stewards live by the Law of Personal Initiative and choose willingly to give our all for Him?

LIVING THE LAWS

The call to discipleship is a call to stewardship. It is not meant to be easy, nor is it always filled with pleasure. In fact, it is often difficult and incessantly demanding. Every step of the way it requires personal choice, for to do His will we must exercise our own. There are innumerable ways in which we can proactively meet the challenge of choice. Here are three:

Take the initiative in giving to the plight of the poor. Read the Gospels and consider the attitude Jesus had toward the poor. He felt deep compassion for them, He loved them, He healed them, He related to them without partiality. Granted, the world in which Jesus lived couldn't be much different from the comfortable suburban lifestyle most of us know today. He encountered the poor every day, whereas most American Christians seldom if ever relate to the poor and downtrodden. Of course, there are poor people in our society, but they're conveniently hidden from view. What then can we do to love them and help them with Christ-like concern? We can pray for them, of course, but that won't put food in their stomachs or a roof over their heads. The need is best met through giving money, giving time and giving care in the name of Jesus. Seek the Lord, ask how He would have you do this, then follow however He leads.

Take the initiative in giving to the cause of Christ. Dr. Donald Barnhouse, a godly pastor of the 20th century, wrote on this subject: "If by our giving souls may be saved on the other side of the world, if by our giving young people may be saved who then carry the torch of truth into the next generation, then when our control of money fails, when death relaxes our hold upon the possessions to which we have so tightly held, we shall find on the other side in the presence of God those whom we have blessed with our gifts, the souls who have been reached through all we have expended for the Lord, those who have been blessed through the teaching of the Word because we gave — these will be there to welcome us in reception to our reward." Jesus put it like this: "I tell you, use worldly wealth to gain friends for yourselves, so that when it is gone, you will be welcomed into eternal dwellings."[3]

Take the initiative in giving to the spread of the Gospel. Jesus is not a way, a truth, a life. He is the only Way, the only Truth, the only Life — and no one comes to the Father except through Him. By giving for the sake of the Gospel we are ensuring that the message goes forth. No priority of stewardship is more important.

Scripture References:
[1] 2 Corinthians 8:3
[2] Matthew 10:8
[3] Luke 16:9

16

THE LAW OF
TOTAL EXCELLENCE

Excellence in giving is part of a matched set of virtues.

Collectors can become obsessive about acquiring an entire set. It may be a particular year of baseball cards, or a specific issue of stamps, or a certain set of ceramic figurines; whatever it may be, getting all the pieces is the goal. There's a unique satisfaction that comes from having something complete and perfectly connected.

In the Apostle Paul's second letter to the believers in Corinth, he describes a complete set of ideals, and he urges them to have the whole collection as it were: "But just as you excel in everything — in faith, in speech, in knowledge, in complete earnestness and in your love for us — see that you also excel in this grace of giving."[1] This verse describes a matched set of virtues, a combination of qualities that epitomize all that is best: excellence in what one believes, says, knows, desires, feels and gives. For the believer, living with this kind of excellence is paramount, for it reflects the pure perfection of God.

Excellence should characterize the servant of Jesus Christ, and it should be thoroughly evident in our stewardship. The Law of Total Excellence reinforces this priority, teaching us to always pursue the highest and best, never settling for mediocrity. Take a look at the men and women of faith in Scripture and it's crystal clear that they were people who excelled. Consider Daniel, for example, who impressed everyone with his wisdom, knowledge and discernment. The Bible says that Daniel had "a spirit of excellence"[2] in him. His commitment to God and commitment to excellence ran so deep that he was able to achieve astonishing success.

> Many Christians, unfortunately, settle for the easy road.
> They choose the acceptable over the exceptional, the paved highway over the rugged trail. However, those who choose the way of excellence experience the greatest views and the most memorable journey.

Above all, Daniel never forgot his faith or failed his God. Against the odds and in spite of the people who didn't want him to succeed, he kept going. Their jealousy and evil plots against him were formidable, threatening his very life. But Daniel would not give in, nor would he alter his spiritual habits. His "spirit of excellence" would not allow him to keep his faith a secret, and just as he had always done, he opened his windows toward Jerusalem, got down on his knees, and prayed to God. Predictably, Daniel's enemies brought charges against him and presented the undeniable evidence of his "crime." The king, entrapped by his own decree, was forced to throw Daniel into a den of ravenous lions. But the story was far from over: God miraculously shut the lions' mouths and spared Daniel from certain death. The greatly relieved king ordered that Daniel be brought up out of the pit and that all of his accusers be thrown to the wild animals instead.[3]

Daniel excelled in good times and bad. Regardless of the circumstances, he was the same person, a man of faith who would not be limited by "normal" expectations. He had learned, as all believers must learn, that the way of excellence is often a difficult path. Most people and, unfortunately, many Christians, settle for the easy road. They choose the acceptable over the exceptional, the paved highway over the rugged trail. However, those who choose the way of excellence experience the greatest views and the most memorable journey.

LIVING THE LAWS

To excel in the grace of giving is very demanding. It demands spiritual discipline, personal determination and unconditional devotion. But the rewards are great when you endeavor to do God's will with all your heart and soul.

Discipline yourself to give. Sometimes it's hard to give, especially when what you're giving cost a lot to acquire. Working hard to earn a good income requires discipline, to be sure, but the very ability to do a job comes from God in the first place. He is the great enabler, the one who gives us the strength to work, and He will give us as well the strength to give. The choice is ours, and the discipline of consistent, committed contribution to His purposes is our challenge.

Determine to give daily. One of God's most assuring promises is to give us each day our daily bread. Of course, this means much more than a loaf of bread; it's symbolic of the whole scope of His blessings and providence. Everything that comes to us, every day of our lives, is a gift of his grace. His desire is that we respond to that grace with grace — the grace of giving. We must make this determination on a daily, continuing basis.

Devote yourself to the Giver. Above all, giving is an act of devotion, an expression of worship. God is the perfect and infinite giver, and when we give we are imitating His character. Giving to the Lord's work is a test of love because we worship what we love. As Jesus taught in the Sermon on the Mount, "Do not store up for yourselves treasures on earth, where moth and rust destroy, and where thieves break in and steal. But store up for yourselves treasures in heaven, where moth and rust do not destroy, and where thieves do not break in and steal. For where your treasure is, there your heart will be also."[4] If our hearts belong to God, our treasure in all its forms will be devoted to Him.

The goal in striving for excellence is not to attain perfection but to achieve quality — the highest quality of which one is capable. It is a never-ending endeavor to please God and give to Him without reservation.

Scripture References:
[1] 2 Corinthians 8:7
[2] Daniel 5:12
[3] Daniel 6:1-28
[4] Matthew 6:19-21

17

THE LAW OF
RIGHTFUL REWARD

*Reward for stewardship and service is
granted by God, not gained by man.*

A rich young man had come to Jesus seeking the key to
life. He had been moral and upright, but he knew
something was missing. "What do I still lack?" he asked. Jesus
answered him, "Go, sell your possessions and give to the poor,
and you will have treasure in heaven. Then come, follow me."
But upon hearing this, he went away very sad because he was
very wealthy. As the young man left, Jesus said to his disciples,
"I tell you the truth, it is hard for a rich man to enter the kingdom of heaven. Again I tell you, it is easier for a camel to go
through the eye of a needle than for a rich man to enter the
kingdom of God."[1]

Impetuous Peter sized up the situation and blurted out,
"We have left everything to follow you! What then will there
be for us?" Jesus replied, "Everyone who has left houses or
brothers or sisters or father or mother or children or fields for
my sake will receive a hundred times as much and will inherit
eternal life. But many who are first will be last, and many who
are last will be first."[2] And, while the disciples were still

contemplating that idea, Jesus launched into an intriguing parable to further illustrate the point:

"For the kingdom of heaven is like a landowner who went out early in the morning to hire laborers for his vineyard. Now when he had agreed with the laborers for a denarius a day, he sent them into his vineyard. And he went out about the third hour and saw others standing idle in the marketplace, and said to them, 'You also go into the vineyard, and whatever is right I will give you.' So they went. Again he went out about the sixth and the ninth hour, and did likewise. And about the eleventh hour he went out and found others standing idle, and said to them, 'Why have you been standing here idle all day?' They said to him, 'Because no one hired us.' He said to them, 'You also go into the vineyard, and whatever is right you will receive.' So when evening had come, the owner of the vineyard said to his steward, 'Call the laborers and give them their wages, beginning with the last to the first.' And when those came who were hired about the eleventh hour, they each received a denarius. But when the first came, they supposed that they would receive more; and they likewise received each a denarius. And when they had received it, they complained against the landowner, saying, 'These last men have worked only one hour, and you made them equal to us who have borne the burden and the heat of the day.' But he answered one of them and said, 'Friend, I am doing you no wrong. Did you not agree with me for a denarius? Take what is yours and go your way. I wish to give to this last man the same as to you. Is it not lawful for me to do what I wish with my own things? Or is your eye evil because I am good?' So the last will be first, and the first last."[3]

In Jesus' day there were no labor organizations or unions. Day laborers gathered in the town marketplace early in the morning, waiting and hoping to be hired. The average pay for a day's work was a denarius, a Roman coin sufficient to purchase basic necessities. The landowner, anxious to get his harvest in before the rains, went to the labor pool at six in the morning and recruited some workers. The harvest was great, and the laborers were few, so he returned at 9:00, at noon and at 3:00 in the afternoon. At 5:00 he still needed workers, so he hired yet another group.

The men hired early in the day would not go to work until they knew how much they would make. The other workers had no contract. They trusted the owner to give them what was right. The owner paid the men in reverse order, so that the 6:00 a.m. group would see how generous he was to those who did not have a contract. The first group of men complained, of course, but what they received was exactly what they had bargained for.

> God does not limit Himself to what is just and equal; He gives what is gracious and generous. We should therefore never be anxious about our reward or afraid of God's will, for He will always do what is best for us.

The principle of stewardship at work in Jesus' teaching is the Law of Rightful Reward. He is establishing the fact that *rewards for stewardship and service are granted by God, not gained by man.* We must trust the Lord and rely on His Word and His character. After all, God does not limit Himself to what is just and equal; He gives what is gracious and generous.

We should therefore never be anxious about our reward or afraid of God's will, for He will always do what is best for us if we simply obey Him with the right heart attitude.

LIVING THE LAWS

Beware of making bargains with God. Let's go back to Peter's question that prompted Jesus' parable. Peter had asked, what are we going to get out of this? In essence, he wanted to "sign a contract" with the Lord. In his brilliant reply, Jesus implies, Why not trust me to give you what is right? The lesson for us is clear: don't make bargains with God. If we write the contract, we will always be losers. However, if we let Him take care of us, we will receive "exceedingly abundantly above all we could ask or think."[4]

Beware of watching others. The contrast between the rich young man and the disciples is quite interesting. Some of them had given up good professions to follow Jesus, but the wealthy man had given up nothing. Yet he was still rich and they were now poor! Surely, they thought, there must be some kind of compensation coming. Peter (and probably most of the other disciples) were guilty of watching other people, and that's a dangerous business. When we get our eyes off the Lord and start watching others, certain symptoms start showing up in our lives. We start to envy them and what they have. We start to get what Jesus called "an evil eye" that keeps us from seeing anything good in them. We start comparing, coveting and complaining. The end result is bitterness toward God, like the "raw deal" syndrome that affected the elder brother in the parable of the prodigal son. Bitterness robs us of the joy of God's blessings, and we must diligently avoid it.

Beware of overconfidence. The workers in the parable were overconfident because of what they deemed their work to be worth. Peter and the disciples were overconfident because they focused on what they saw as sacrificial living. "We have left everything to follow you!" Peter said. Peter thought he was among the first, but Jesus warned that he might find himself the last. As the Apostle Paul cautioned, "Judge nothing before the appointed time; wait till the Lord comes. He will bring to light what is hidden in darkness and will expose the motives of men's hearts. At that time, each will receive his praise from God."[5] Overconfidence always results in disappointment because our judgments are bound to be faulty since we do not see men's hearts. It is the motive that determines the value of the ministry, and there will be many surprises when Christ judges.

Living by the Law of Rightful Reward is critical to maintaining spiritual balance. We can be confident that God will give us far more than we deserve but we must not serve Him only for reward. Most importantly, we must watch our motives and be sure we serve God because of one thing primarily — our love for Him.

Scripture References:
[1] Matthew 19:16-26
[2] Matthew 19:27-30
[3] Matthew 20:1-16
[4] Ephesians 3:20
[5] 1 Corinthians 4:5

18

THE LAW OF
ZEALOUS READINESS

Zealous stewardship spreads like a powerful contagion.

His name was Simon, but we know him better by the descriptor that follows his name: the Zealot. Unlike his famous namesake, Simon Peter, who became the most prominent of the Twelve Apostles, Simon the Zealot is virtually unknown to us. Not a single word he ever said or a single deed he ever did is recorded in the Scriptures. The only thing the Bible tells us about Simon is that he was a Zealot. Yet, in this one potent word we can see a man of flaming enthusiasm. Like the peephole in a wooden fence through which one can view a vast landscape, this word "Zealot" reveals a great deal to us.

In Jesus' day, the Zealots were a loosely-structured organization of what we would today call guerrilla fighters. They were fiercely committed to liberating Palestine from Roman tyranny, and those who joined with the Zealots had to go through a "conversion" experience, selling themselves out to the cause. As a Zealot, Simon had to be a certain kind of person. He had to be an idealist, thinking his side could actually win. He had to be a visionary, looking ahead to the liberation of his people. He had to be sincere, believing the cause to be right. And he had to be dedicated, so dedicated that he would willingly give his life in the struggle.

When Simon put his faith in Jesus and accepted Him as Messiah, he abandoned his old commitment and embraced a completely new one. He had found something more important than the cause; indeed, he had found the One whom the Jewish people had for centuries longed for: the Christ. He had met the true Liberator, and nothing would ever be the same. Simon did not cease to be the zealous, impassioned person he was before; rather, he discovered a entirely new focus for that zealousness and passion. From that point forward, his life was dedicated to service and stewardship as a disciple of Jesus Christ. According to first century historians, Simon ultimately gave his life for Christ, dying as a martyr for his Lord.

> True Christianity is not of this earth but of heaven. It is not temporal but eternal. It is not bound by the natural, but is lived within the supernatural boundaries of God's grace. True Christianity belongs to another level, another dimension. It is life on a different plane.

Simon personified the Law of Zealous Readiness which is described by Paul in the first verses of 2 Corinthians 9: "There is no need for me to write to you about this service to the saints," he begins, "for I know your eagerness to help, and I have been boasting about it to the Macedonians, telling them that since last year you in Achaia were ready to give; and your enthusiasm has stirred most of them to action."[1] Godly zeal is a powerful force which has a contagious effect on other believers. When the Corinthian Christians gave eagerly and enthusiastically it motivated the Macedonians to do likewise.

To be zealously ready as a servant and steward of Jesus Christ is to live with a heightened sense of responsiveness to God's leading. It is not to be fanatical but to be radical, for true Christianity *is* radical because it is a life lived in radical opposition to all the forces of the world, the flesh and the devil. True Christianity belongs neither to the left nor to the right in the political realm. True Christianity is neither conservative nor liberal in the social realm. True Christianity is not of this earth but of heaven. It is not temporal but eternal. It is not bound by the natural, but is lived within the supernatural boundaries of God's grace. True Christianity belongs to another level, another dimension. It is life on a different plane.

Sometimes Christians become fanatical, going off on tangents or giving their time and energies to causes rather than to Christ. Such fanatical behavior is usually prompted either by a misunderstanding of God's Word, misapplication of God's truth or sin in some area of life that has created the need for a spiritual smokescreen. But the zealously ready steward is motivated by the pure desire to use every resource to please God and fulfill His purposes.

The Law of Zealous Readiness confirms that enthusiasm is a good thing if it is directed toward a godly purpose. The purpose of fanaticism is the cause or activity or idea itself. The purpose of Christian zeal, however, is a Person, Christ Himself. "I am the gate,"[2] Jesus said categorically. The essence of Christianity is not a cause, a philosophy, a religion or an idea. It is a Person. Who He is, what He has done, why He is. These are the things that truly matter.

LIVING THE LAWS

In the context of biblical stewardship, zealousness is a Christ-centered passion to give everything for His sake. It is all-encompassing, enfolding all that one is capable of giving: money, time, influence, help, counsel or a thousand-and-one other things. The motive behind the giving is the indwelling love of Christ. "For Christ's love compels us,"[3] Paul explained in his second letter to the Corinthians. Whereas the religious fanatics of today's world are motivated by anger, guilt or fear, the believer is compelled by love. Having been set free from the penalty of sin we are now enabled to live in triumph over the power of sin. In this regard, the zealous Christian experiences a victory that is profoundly spiritual.

See only Christ as the Cause. When Simon joined the Zealots he probably had no reservations. Most likely, he gave himself wholly to the cause. But then he learned of the One greater than any cause, the Lord Jesus Christ. Still a zealous man, Simon redirected his zeal to serve the only one worth serving. His instructions came directly from the Lord, who taught him what it meant to be a disciple. He heard it when Jesus said, "If anyone would come after me, he must deny himself and take up his cross and follow me."[4] He was there when Jesus said, "Any of you who does not give up everything he has cannot be my disciple."[5] And he was listening when the Lord said, "I tell you the truth, no one who has left home or brothers or sisters or mother or father or children or fields for me and the gospel will fail to receive a hundred times as much in this present age...and in the age to come, eternal life."[6] Simon was listening, and he took the words to heart, as indeed we should.

Count only Christ as dear. As we put into practice the Laws of Stewardship there is an ever-growing realization that these are Laws of Discipleship as well, for stewardship is inextricably linked to discipleship. To be a disciple is to be a steward; to be a steward is to be a disciple. In both respects (as disciples and as stewards), our priority is not ourselves but the Lord. Forsaking everything else, we count only Christ as dear. With zealous readiness, we say with Paul, "I consider my life worth nothing to me, if only I may finish the race and complete the task the Lord Jesus has given me — the task of testifying to the gospel of God's grace."[7]

Scripture References:
[1] 2 Corinthians 9:1-2
[2] John 10:9
[3] 2 Corinthians 5:14
[4] Mark 8:34
[5] Luke 14: 33
[6] Mark 10:29-30
[7] Acts 20:24

19

THE LAW OF GRACEFUL ABUNDANCE

Abundant grace brings abundant blessing and spurs abundant ministry.

At first glance they appeared to be just a pile of rocks. But their significance was great, for they represented God's blessing upon an entire nation. Joshua had instructed the people to carry twelve large stones from the bed of the Jordan River and place them on the Canaan side in a place called Gilgal. Arranged together, the stones formed a memorial to God's power in stopping the flow of the Jordan so that the people could cross over into the promised land. In subsequent years, the Israelites would periodically return to Gilgal to express their gratitude for victories won in their new land. On those important occasions they were to bring their children, so that no one would forget God's abundant grace upon them. Joshua said to them, "In the future, when your children ask you, 'What do these stones mean?' tell them that the flow of the Jordan was cut off before the ark of the covenant of the Lord. When it crossed the Jordan, the waters of the Jordan were cut off. These stones are to be a memorial to the people of Israel forever."[1]

Whenever the people of Israel obeyed God's instruction regarding the twelve stones, it provided a marvelous opportunity to instruct the next generation. A child's natural curiosity opens the door to describe God's remarkable power. And adults as well benefit from remembering what God has done. Recalling His abundant grace, the believer is encouraged and motivated to respond in worship and service. *God's abundant grace brings abundant blessing and spurs abundant ministry.* This is a basic principle of stewardship, the Law of Graceful Abundance. Paul explained it like this: "And God is able to make all grace abound to you, so that in all things at all times, having all that you need, you will abound in every good work."[2]

> God's promise is limitless: He is able to make *all* grace abound toward us. His grace is relevant in *all* things at *all* times. He will provide *all* that we need. He will enable us to abound in *every* good work. There is no reason under any circumstances for us as believers to ever feel spiritually limited.

God's promise is limitless: He is able to make *all* grace abound toward us. His grace is relevant in *all* things at *all* times. He will provide *all* that we need. He will enable us to abound in *every* good work. There is no reason under any circumstances for us as believers to ever feel spiritually limited. Those two words alone — *all* and *every* — should be sufficient reminders of His power at work in us and for us.

If you want to be encouraged about God's power, look at the earthly ministry of Jesus. Consider the ways in which He transformed lives and remember that His power is still at work in us today. Think about the time that he encountered a demon-possessed man in the region of the Gerasenes. So tormented was the man that no one was able to subdue him, even with chains, and he spent night and day wandering among the tombs, crying out and cutting himself with sharp stones. Jesus asked him, "What is your name?" And the man replied, "My name is Legion, for we are many."[3] Actually, it was the numerous demons within the man replying. Jesus then cast out the demons, sending them into a herd of 2,000 pigs which promptly rushed into a nearby lake and drowned. The incident attracted much attention and people from the area came to see what had happened. "When they came to Jesus, they saw the man who had been possessed by the legion of demons, sitting there, dressed and in his right mind; and they were afraid."[4] A display of such spiritual power can be frightening, but its purpose is pure. Jesus told the man who had been set free from the demons, "Go home to your family and tell them how much the Lord has done for you, and how he has had mercy on you."[5]

Go and tell others how much the Lord has done for you. What a simple, powerful reminder this is to each of us to testify of all that God is doing in us. Private thanksgiving is important, but it is incomplete without a public acknowledgement of God's goodness. Communicating our gratitude to God is crucial because it makes us more reliant on the Lord and it has a profoundly positive effect on those around us. Thankfulness occurs inwardly, in what our heart expresses. Glorifying God happens publicly, in what our mouth confesses. Public expressions of gratitude for God's grace strengthen our commitment to Him while counteracting our human tendencies to self-sufficiency and self-reliance. After all, our successes are not of our own making; they are the result of what God is doing in us and we are merely beneficiaries.

LIVING THE LAWS

We are stewards of God's abundant blessings, guardians of all that He has done and is doing in our lives. Our priority is to manage these unique resources with thankfulness and thoughtfulness.

Build a memorial of gratitude for God's grace. We're not suggesting that you build an actual structure, but a written memorial of the ways in which God's abundant grace have resulted in abundant blessings in your life. The "stones" in your memorial are the great events and experiences through which God has taken you on your spiritual journey. As you remember each one, your appreciation will grow as your motivation in ministry grows.

Tell how much the Lord has done for you. You are the only steward of the story that only you can tell. No one else can give a first-person account of what God is doing to guide you, provide for you, empower you and bless you as you serve Him. Be a faithful witness.

Scripture References:
[1] Joshua 4:6-7
[2] 2 Corinthians 9:8
[3] Mark 5:9
[4] Mark 5:15
[5] Mark 5:19

20

THE LAW OF
SECRET SPIRITUALITY
*Godly giving is a private demonstration,
not a public display.*

A braham had to wait a quarter of a century — 25 long years — before the promised son was born. By then he was 100 years old; his wife, Sarah, was 90. Yet God superceded the laws of nature to allow the birth of a child to an elderly, barren couple. They named their son Isaac, meaning "laughter," because he brought unspeakable joy to them.

After Isaac had grown into young manhood, God commanded Abraham to give an extraordinary offering: "Take your son, your only son, Isaac, whom you love, and go to the region of Moriah. Sacrifice him there as a burnt offering on one of the mountains I will tell you about."[1]

Obediently, Abraham took his boy on that long, agonizing trip to the bleak slopes of Moriah. Though he did not comprehend God's purpose, Abraham's faith was not shaken. He complied with the instructions, placing his dear son on the altar and raising a knife to plunge into the young man's chest. At the very moment he lifted the knife to slay his son, God stopped him. The Lord commanded Abraham to sacrifice instead a ram which was caught in a nearby bush.

We wonder: Would he have gone through with it? Would the old man have actually offered his own beloved son? The Bible gives us the answer: "Abraham reasoned that God could raise the dead, and figuratively speaking, he did receive Isaac back from death."[2] Yes, he would have done it, for he was already expecting God to raise his son from the dead!

> With rare exceptions, giving is to be a private demonstration of obedience, not a public display of magnanimity. God is pleased when a gift is given with regard only for the Lord, completely devoid of any attention being drawn to the giver.

No one was anywhere nearby when Abraham and Isaac were on that mountain. The offering to be given that day was a private offering, seen only by God. There in that remarkable situation so many centuries ago, a principle of stewardship was revealed: the Law of Secret Spirituality. It's the same principle we discover in the words of Jesus: "Be careful not to do your acts of righteousness before men, to be seen by them. If you do, you will have no reward from your Father in heaven. So when you give...do not announce it with trumpets, as the hypocrites do in the synagogues and on the streets, to be honored by men. I tell you the truth, they have received their reward in full... Do not let your left hand know what your right hand is doing, so that your giving may be in secret. Then your Father, who sees what is done in secret, will reward you."[3]

LIVING THE LAWS

With rare exceptions, giving is to be a private demonstration of obedience, not a public display of magnanimity. God is pleased when a gift is given with regard only for the Lord, completely devoid of any attention being drawn to the giver. To draw attention to oneself when giving is to express an attitude of ownership rather than stewardship. If you think that what you are giving is something you own instead of something that has been entrusted to you, you have eliminated God from the equation. The wise steward never forgets that everything belongs to God and every gift is facilitated by Him alone.

Don't draw attention to yourself; direct attention to the Lord. The Law of Secret Spirituality reminds us that righteous giving is God-centered, not man-centered. To give in order to impress others with how spiritual we are actually denies our spirituality, and it is an affront to God. The believer's concern should never be with what people think but with what God thinks. If we live in a way that honors Him and gives Him glory, we don't have to worry about what people think. The one takes care of the other.

Don't measure yourself against other Christians. The standard we are to measure by is the character of Christ, not the character of other Christians. Paul had to address this problem in writing to the Corinthians: "We do not dare to classify or compare ourselves with some who commend themselves. When they measure themselves by themselves and compare themselves with themselves, they are not wise."[4] Peer pressure must not prompt one to give. The prompting of the Holy Spirit is to be our guide.

Don't forget the faith factor. The heart of Spirit-directed giving is faith. At the core of Abraham's willingness to give his own son was unbounded faith in the One who gave that son in the first place. As the Word says, "Faith is being sure of what we hope for and certain of what we do not see."[5] In order to tap the endless resources of God, the believer must exercise faith by acting in obedience to God's Word. Paul explained to the Romans: "Faith comes by hearing, and hearing by the Word of God."[6] When one is prompted to give either by the Word of God or by the leadership of the Spirit, obedience to that prompting is an expression of true spirituality.

Scripture References:
[1] Genesis 22:2
[2] Hebrews 11:19
[3] Matthew 6:1-4
[4] 2 Corinthians 10:12
[5] Hebrews 11:1
[6] Romans 10:17

21

THE LAW OF SACRIFICIAL EXAMPLE

The most significant gifts are often given by the most insignificant givers.

He sat down opposite the collection area and watched intently as the offerings were given. People from all walks of life were entering the courtyard to make their contributions to the temple treasury. Among the crowd were a number of rich people who threw in large amounts of money. Undoubtedly some gave with a flourish that drew attention to their great generosity. But then He spotted her, a lowly widow who entered humbly and put in two very small copper coins, worth only a fraction of a penny. Calling His disciples to him, Jesus said, "I tell you the truth, this poor widow has put more into the treasury than all the others. They gave out of their wealth; but she, out of her poverty, put in everything — all she had to live on."[1]

Everyone else had given out of their abundance, but she gave her all. In one simple act she demonstrated true sacrifice, proven not just by what she put in, but by what she had left over. She epitomized the Law of Sacrificial Example, showing that *the most significant gifts are often given by the most insignificant givers.* It's doubtful that anyone but Jesus actually noticed her that day, but God is paying attention and He sees things no one else sees and interprets meaning no one else grasps. What matters to Him is wholehearted devotion, and what pleases Him is the exercise of genuine faith. The poor widow was wholly devoted to God, willing by faith to give everything. She loved the Lord with an absolute love, and He would bless her for that consecration to Him.

What God desires of us as stewards is that we live by a philosophy of life that reflects His character. Jesus gave a potent illustration of this when He was asked by a young Jewish lawyer, "Teacher, what must I do to inherit eternal life?" Jesus answered with a question of His own: "What is written in the Law? How do you read it?" The lawyer replied, quoting Scripture: "Love the Lord your God will all your heart and with all your soul and with all your strength and with all your mind, and Love your neighbor as yourself." To this, Jesus said, "You have answered correctly. Do this and you will live." But the man wasn't satisfied with Jesus' answer, and he asked, "And who is my neighbor?"[2] In reply, Jesus told a story that is among the best known of all His teachings, the parable of the Good Samaritan.[3] In that unforgettable account, Jesus reveals three essential philosophies of life:

The first philosophy says, *"What's yours is mine."*

The second says, *"What's mine is mine."*

The third philosophy expresses the belief that *"What's mine is yours."*

The first philosophy – *What's Yours is Mine* – is shown through the behavior of thieves who attack a defenseless man on the road to Jericho. They beat him mercilessly, strip off his clothing, steal all his belongings and leave him naked and bleeding at the roadside.

A short time later, two "religious" men, a priest and a Levite, happen to walk by the scene of the crime. However, they do nothing to help. In fact, they cross the road to avoid getting any closer. Their philosophy – *What's Mine is Mine* – dictates that they mind their own business and do their own thing, regardless of the compelling need.

Finally, someone else, a Samaritan, approaches the dying man; and, unlike the ones who preceded him, he responds in a very different manner. Although he is of a different race, a different religion and a different culture than the injured man, he takes the necessary action. Lovingly, he tends to the man's wounds, pouring in oil and wine. He then loads the man on his own donkey for the arduous 10-mile journey into the city. Upon arriving there, he pays for the wounded man's lodging and care, even promising the innkeeper to pay more, if necessary.

LIVING THE LAWS

The Samaritan's philosophy – *What's Mine is Yours* – permeates his actions and his attitudes. His behavior sets an example we are to follow today as we live out the Law of Sacrificial Example in our stewardship. Our challenge is to look at our lives and ask honestly, what would God have me give sacrificially for His sake? There are people in desperate need today — physically, emotionally, and spiritually desperate — and God uses people to meet such needs. As the Samaritan's actions saved a man's life, we too can be instruments used of God in His miraculous work of redemption. As true believers it is imperative that we look at all of our resources and say resoundingly, *Lord, What's Mine is Yours!* This must be our philosophy, for without this spirit of sacrifice we cannot and will not mature and succeed spiritually.

When your church has a major need, give sacrificially to meet it. As a member of the body, your participation is crucial, especially at time of special need. Whether it is for a new building, a debt retirement project or some other kind of ministry expansion, your sacrificial involvement will be a blessing both personally and corporately.

When your neighbor has a major problem, give sacrificially to solve it. Be a Samaritan, and be open to what is going on in the lives around you. Be sensitive to what's happening with them and be responsive in the ways that you are able. It may demand the sacrifice of time more than money, of emotional energy more than financial assistance; but whatever it takes, be an instrument of Christ's love.

When your Christian brothers and sisters have a major crisis, give sacrificially to confront it. Think, for example, about believers who are being persecuted for their faith, many of them punished for the "crime" of serving Jesus. Their sacrifice is an inspiration to us, and it should also motivate us to sacrifice, too, with "Good Samaritan" gifts on their behalf.

Only you know the meaning of "sacrifice" in your life. Whatever it is, pray earnestly that God would enable you to serve Him and give to Him in a truly sacrificial manner.

Scripture References:
[1] Mark 12:43-44
[2] Luke 10:25-29
[3] Luke 10:30-37

22

THE LAW OF
OVER-THE-TOP OFFERINGS
Blessed believers live and give above and beyond.

T his is a tale of two offerings.

Both offerings were for the purpose of funding the construction of extraordinary places of worship — a grand Tabernacle and a great Temple.

Both offerings were taken by extraordinary men of God — one by Moses, the other by King David.

Both offerings required the extraordinary involvement of God's people giving of their money, their time, their skills, their possessions and their unbridled energy.

These two offerings were given under very different circumstances by people who lived in different eras, hundreds of years apart. But the similarities are striking, especially in the wholehearted response to a formidable challenge.

The first offering, given by the nation of Israel for the building of the Tabernacle, was utterly unique. No project like it had ever been done in the annals of human history, and the architect was none other than God Himself, who revealed the plans to the prophet Moses. Everything about the Tabernacle was distinctive: exotic woods, spectacular fabrics, elaborately symbolic furnishings, even special garments for the priests to wear while inside the structure. Building it was a demanding, complex task. But the people rose to the occasion: "Then Moses summoned...every skilled person to whom the Lord had given ability and who was willing to come and do the work. They received from Moses all the offerings the Israelites had brought to carry out the work of constructing the sanctuary. And the people continued to bring freewill offerings morning after morning."[1]

The people were giving and giving, so much in fact that their response was overwhelming: "So all the skilled craftsmen who were doing all the work on the sanctuary left their work and said to Moses, 'The people are bringing more than enough for doing the work the Lord commanded to be done.'"[2] That's right: they gave more than was needed! It was an unheard-of "crisis" and Moses had to intervene: "Then Moses gave an order and they sent this word throughout the camp: 'No man or woman is to make anything else as an offering for the sanctuary.' And so the people were restrained from bringing more, because what they already had was more than enough to do all the work."[3]

Imagine a pastor today having to say, "Beloved, please don't give any more to the building fund. You've already contributed more than we need." It's very doubtful that we'll ever hear those words, and it underscores what a phenomenal response the people of Israel made.

In the offering received by King David, the project was different yet nonetheless distinctive. In fact, it was the most captivatingly beautiful building ever to be constructed, a palatial structure dedicated to God. David personally set the example in giving to the offering: "With all my resources I have provided for the temple of my God — gold for the gold work, silver for the silver, bronze for the bronze, iron for the iron and wood for the wood, as well as onyx for the settings, turquoise, stones of various colors, and all kinds of fine stone and marble — all of these in large quantities." And he wasn't done, even with that extravagant generosity. "Besides," he said, "in my devotion to the temple of my God I now give my personal treasures of gold and silver for the temple of my God, over and above everything I have provided for this holy temple."[4] David, being the inspirational and God-honoring leader he was, demonstrated the importance of the offering by giving super-abundantly — an "over and above" contribution.

The people of Israel, inspired by their king's example, gave with great enthusiasm, joyously expressing their commitment. David put it all in perspective: "O Lord our God, as for all this abundance that we have provided for building you a temple for your Holy Name, it comes from your hand, and all of it belongs to you. I know, my God, that you test the heart and are pleased with integrity. All these things have I given willingly and with honest intent. And now I have seen with joy how willingly your people who are here have given to you."[5]

Two offerings, given by different people in different eras, yet so similar in many ways. Both are examples of the Law of Over-the-Top Offerings, the principle which teaches us that *blessed believers live and give above and beyond.* Even though they lived so long ago, we can learn much from the generosity of God's people who participated in the offerings for the Tabernacle and the Temple. Their obedience is exemplary, and we are wise to replicate it in our experience as believers of the 21st century. Here are some ways we can do that:

LIVING THE LAWS

When your church has a major project, get involved in a major way. The contribution of your money is important, of course; but equally valuable (to you and to the church) is the contribution of your unique talents and abilities. Whatever you have to offer, be it money, goods, professional skills or practical advice, be willing to participate in a major way.

When you give to the Lord's work, go above and beyond the call of duty. Don't be a "status quo" Christian, content to simply do and give what's expected. Think outside the box, expand the horizons of your faith and go above and beyond in your giving to the Lord.

When you receive a challenge to give, see it as an opportunity, not an interference. As David reminds all of us, everything comes from God's hand and it all belongs to Him anyway, so how could we see giving as anything but a great opportunity? Let's remember David's prayer for his people and let's make it our own: "O Lord...keep this desire in the hearts of your people forever, and keep their hearts loyal to you."[6]

Scripture References:
[1] Exodus 36:2-3
[2] Exodus 36:4-5
[3] Exodus 36:6-7
[4] 1 Chronicles 29:2-3
[5] 1 Chronicles 29:16-17
[6] 1 Chronicles 29:18

23

THE LAW OF
UNIFIED COMMITMENT

Oneness of heart and mind
brings greatness of power and witness.

You probably don't know who Theodore Maiman is, but his scientific developments are an important element of your daily life. Dr. Maiman perfected the first commercially viable laser. His breakthrough device was a small rod made of ruby crystals which was set inside a cylinder. At either end of the cylinder is affixed a mirror, one end fully reflective and the other only partially silvered so that a strong light can pass through. Through a flash tube coiled around the cylinder, flashes of light are fired into the rod. The atoms along the rod then become "excited" and produce tiny bursts of light called photons. These photons collide with the atoms, exciting them to produce more and more photons until the tube is filled with them bouncing back and forth from mirror to mirror. The amount of photons becomes so great that they pass right through the partially reflective mirror. This is the laser beam.

A medium-powered laser and a medium-wattage light bulb can actually have the same number of photons. However, the light bulb has the strength only to warm one's hand while the laser can cut through steel. Why such a huge difference? In the light bulb, the photons keep bouncing around randomly. In the laser, they line up, unifying to produce phenomenal power. The difference lies in the strength of unity.

In the spiritual realm, unity produces great power as well. When believers unify, the result is potent. Take the example of the Christians on the Day of Pentecost, shortly after Jesus had ascended to heaven. The Book of Acts tells us that "All the believers were one in heart and mind. No one claimed that any of his possessions was his own, but they shared everything they had. With great power the apostles continued to testify to the resurrection of the Lord Jesus, and much grace was upon them all."[1] They were unified in heart and mind. They were unified in their attitude toward material possessions. They were unified in testifying to Christ's resurrection truth. And in their unity they experienced "great power."

When believers unite to give, as those first Christians gave, an undeniable power results. This is a basic precept of stewardship, the Law of Unified Commitment. It's the law which teaches us how *oneness of heart and mind brings greatness of power and witness.* When an offering must be taken, for example, the more unified the participants, the more powerful the impact. God's design and His desire is that we work in spiritual partnership, not as sole proprietors. "Lone rangers" cannot experience the exhilaration of spiritual unity.

Earlier in the same chapter of Acts, we read of the bold ministry of Peter and John and the price they paid for proclaiming the message of Jesus. Because they would not keep quiet about their Lord...because they were convinced that their silence would carry eternal consequences...because their faith was in the One whose Name is above all others...they didn't give up or give in. Although the authorities demanded that they cease to teach about Jesus or even to speak His name, they refused and were put in prison. They remained united in their determination and commitment, and it had the effect of a spiritual laser cutting straight through the heart of a godless culture.[2]

When Peter and John were released from jail, they returned to their fellow Christians and joined them in prayer and fellowship. All the believers recognized the risks they were taking, but in the larger context, the threats didn't matter. Consequently, their prayers were not filled with expressions of anxiety; instead, they overflowed with the promises of Scripture. Their emotions and thoughts were anchored in the reality of who God is. No one pretended that the circumstances were pleasant, but everyone confessed two essential truths — that God is sovereign and that He is forever the Creator. They were absolutely, resolutely unified in these truths.

The same God to whom those first century disciples devoted their lives, that same Sovereign Lord and Creator, is our God. And when we serve Him in unity we are actively confiding in the One who is greater than the one who dominates this world's system. In response to our faithful service, He can create new dispositions in the hearts of our opponents. He can create a thirst for Jesus in the hearts of those who once rejected the Gospel. He can create new circumstances to override the prevailing circumstances. And He can do all this because He is greater than all.

LIVING THE LAWS

Practically speaking, how can we live by the Law of Unified Commitment? Here are three effective ways:

Think of fellow Christians as your partners. To perceive others as partners is to perceive yourself as a partner, and that's a good thing spiritually. Paul was thankful to other Christians for their "partnership in the Gospel"[3] as they united with him in prayer, in work and in financial support. Partnership has numerous beneficial effects and enables us to experience the power of unity.

Think of your gifts to the Lord's work as contributions to a unique mutual fund. In the financial realm, mutual funds incorporate the contributions of thousands of individuals who have pooled their monies to share in the benefits of something very large. In the spiritual realm, all that we give for the Lord's sake is an investment in God's mutual fund, and it pays dividends beyond imagination.

Think of your church as a laser, not a light bulb. When a congregation is truly united in service and stewardship, the impact is powerful. It's like a steel-cutting laser versus a dim-watted light bulb. Unity in spirit and purpose turns a body of believers into a force for righteousness.

Scripture References:
[1] Acts 4:32-33
[2] Acts 4:1-31
[3] Philippians 1:5

24

THE LAW OF
RISKY MISMANAGEMENT
Trying to trick God will always trip you up.

Frank Abagnale was an impressionable 16-year-old when his parents divorced. The judge in their case surprised young Frank by asking him to choose between living with his mother or father. Traumatized and unwilling to choose, Frank ran away to New York City. On his own for the first time, he devised the most ingenious tactics for survival, determining to make his way by sheer force of wit and deception. At six feet tall with prematurely graying hair, Frank already looked a decade older than his true age.

With the small amount of money in his possession, Frank went into a bank to open an account. As a new customer he had to use the generic deposit slips available on the counter, and it gave him a criminally brilliant idea: What if he printed his own account number on the generic deposit slips and returned them to the counter? He decided to try, and the result was more successful than he could have imagined. Every time someone used one of the fake slips, the money was deposited directly into Abagnale's own account. When the bank finally uncovered the crime, Frank had made off with over $40,000.

One deception led to another as Frank became con man extraordinaire. Over the next few years he repeatedly impersonated a Pan Am pilot, flying around the world in the jumpseat of jumbo jets. He forged a Harvard Law diploma, passed the Bar exam, and landed a job in a state attorney general's office. Bored with his "law" career, Frank "became" a pediatrician and was hired as resident supervisor at a Georgia hospital. Taking up the challenge of education, he crafted a fake degree from Columbia University and used it gain a faculty position at Brigham Young University, where he taught sociology for a semester. He also tried his hand as a stockbroker and an FBI agent! Quite impressive for someone without a high school diploma.

Eventually, the real FBI caught up with Frank Abagnale, but not until he had acquired and spent $2.5 million of other people's money. He was tried, convicted and sent to prison, and he remains the most celebrated con man in American history.

Many explanations could be given for Frank Abagnale's behavior. It has been suggested that he was simply reacting to the trauma of his parent's divorce, attempting to please them by incessantly trying to be someone he wasn't. Other experts speculate that Frank had become obsessive and was unable to stop his deception. The fact is that he was a bright, creative, inventive young man, and he was blessed with some extraordinary gifts. However, he deliberately used those gifts in the wrong way.

Two thousand years before Frank Abagnale's sins, a similar deception was practiced by two people who certainly knew better. Unlike their modern counterpart, they professed to be good Christians — so good that they were willing to give sacrificially to the cause of Christ. Or so it seemed. This couple, a husband and wife name Ananias and Sapphira, owned a piece of property which they purportedly sold for the purpose of giving a large offering to the apostles. Unfortunately, they had conspired to keep back part of the money for themselves while pretending to give everything to God. The Apostle Peter saw through the charade: "Ananias," he said, "how is it that Satan has so filled your heart that you have lied to the Holy Spirit and have kept for yourself some of the money you received for the land? Didn't it belong to you before it was sold? And after it was sold, wasn't the money at your disposal? What made you think of doing such a thing? You have not lied to men but to God."[1]

Ananias and Sapphira were trying to cheat God, promising Him everything but only giving Him part. They were violating a basic principle of stewardship, the Law of Risky Mismanagement, which reminds us that *trying to trick God will always trip you up*. Ananias had seen what others in the church were doing: selling their possessions, bringing the money to the leaders, giving sacrificially. He and his wife did not have to sell their property. No one even told them to do it. And, even after they did sell it, they did not have to bring the proceeds to the church. The sin of Ananias and Sapphira was that they decided to hold back part of the purchase price, but give the impression they were giving it all. The money looked so good in their hands, and they agreed upon the scheme. Ananias came down the aisle singing, "I Surrender All" but in his pocket was some of the money. He was lying to the church, yes; but more seriously, he was lying to the Lord.

Peter was led by the Holy Spirit to see through the plot, and the result was a deadly reckoning. When confronted by Peter's convicting questions, Ananias fell down and died. "And great fear seized all who heard what had happened,"[2] the Bible says. But the judgment was not finished. "About three hours later his wife came in, not knowing what had happened. Peter asked her, 'Tell me, is this the price you and Ananias got for the land?' 'Yes,' she said, 'that is the price.' Peter said to her, 'How could you agree to test the Spirit of the Lord? Look! The feet of the men who buried your husband are at the door, and they will carry you out also.' At that moment she fell down at his feet and died. Then the young men came in and, finding her dead, carried her out and buried her beside her husband. Great fear seized the whole church and all who heard about these events."[3] No kidding.

> The money looked so good in their hands, and they agreed upon the scheme. Ananias came down the aisle singing, "I Surrender All" but in his pocket was some of the money. He was lying to the church, yes; but more seriously, he was lying to the Lord.

LIVING THE LAWS

Don't make yourself out to be better than you are. God was teaching the church that He wants a Spirit-led surrender. Nothing fake, nothing contrived; for we have to be honest with Him and with one another. When we mismanage what He has entrusted to us, taking selfish risks with His resources, the consequences can be frightening. It isn't that God is waiting for an opportunity to punish us; but He is watching and He is judging, and we will be held accountable for our stewardship. When we violate His principles, especially when we make ourselves out to be better Christians than we really are, a kind of death occurs — the death that separates us from fellowship with God and with one another.

Engage the great power, experience the great grace, express the great fear. The end and effect of true Christianity is revealed in three key phrases from Acts 4 and 5. The first is "great power." When we live obediently, we have power to witness and power to work for God's glory. The second phrase is "great grace." Grace is, literally, the undeserved, unrecompensed kindness of God. Grace is mercy. It is not some little ingratiated act but is supermagnanimous, for it is undeserved and it cannot be paid back. The third result of true Christianity is bound up in the phrase, "great fear." This fear is a reverential acknowledgement of what God has done. It is the healthy, purifying awareness of God's sovereignty. It's something wise stewards never forget.

Scripture References:
[1] Acts 5:3-4
[2] Acts 5:5
[3] Acts 5:7-11

25

THE LAW OF
HEARTFUL HUMILITY

Putting others first makes an impact that will last.

Early in the 1900s, an American businessman was travelling through Europe by train. Entering his assigned compartment he discovered to his dismay that he was to occupy an uncomfortable upper berth. As he began to complain loudly to the conductor, the young man on the lower berth offered to switch with him. The offer was accepted, and the two men then had a pleasant conversation. The next morning, the young man had to change to another train. "Goodbye," he said to the American traveller, "I hope sometime you will think of Prince Bernadotte. I am on my way to preach the gospel to the Laplanders." The American was stunned. He remembered the news accounts of the young prince who had given up his rights to the throne to become a missionary. Unbeknownst to the businessman, he had been given the better place by the son of Sweden's king!

Excellent stewards consistently choose to put others first, just as Jesus did. They live by the Law of Heartful Humility, disciplining themselves to think outwardly instead of inwardly. Even though they may be remarkable individuals with exceptional skills, they choose not to blow their own horns. Willingly and lovingly, they humble themselves.

The perfect example of heartful humility is, of course, the Lord Jesus Christ, who though He was rich yet for our sake became poor, so that we through His poverty might become rich.[1] And throughout the Bible there are other examples of a humble spirit — servants of God such as Abraham, Jacob, Moses, Joshua, Gideon, Job, Isaiah and Jeremiah. There is John the Baptist, who humbly summarized his life purpose: "He must increase but I must decrease."[2]

> Excellent stewards consistently choose to put others first, just as Jesus did. They live by the Law of Heartful Humility, disciplining themselves to think outwardly instead of inwardly.

Among the most instructive examples of heartful humility is Jonathan, son of King Saul. He understood and practiced this timeless principle, and we can learn much from his life. Jonathan comes first to our attention in 1 Samuel 13:22 when he is described standing in battle with his father. As firstborn son and heir to the throne, Jonathan had already proven his mettle as a bold warrior. We see his courage in telling his armor-bearer, "Come, let's go over to the Philistine outpost on the other side."[3] Without Saul's knowledge, and without informing anyone else, Jonathan and his young lieutenant left the Israelite encampment. On their own, they went into forbidden territory, drew out the enemy forces, fought them in hand-to-hand combat, then witnessed the Philistines' destruction as God sent them into a panic.

Jonathan was blessed with deep spiritual insight. When Jonathan met David, the young shepherd boy who had killed the dread giant, Goliath, "Jonathan became one in spirit with David, and he loved him as he loved himself."[4] Something clicked in Jonathan's heart and mind; and, unlike his self-centered father, Jonathan grasped the biblical principle of respect and was able to discern where the anointing of God was and where it wasn't.

Although they are often thought of as being the same age, Jonathan at the time was about 40 years old and David was a teenager. Yet Jonathan was moved by God to see that his youthful friend was actually the greater leader. "Jonathan made a covenant with David because he loved him as himself. Jonathan took off the robe he was wearing and gave it to David, along with his tunic, and even his sword, his bow and his belt."[5] This was the ultimate expression of Jonathan's heartful humility. Here's what it meant:

In giving his royal robe, his armor, his sword, his bow and his belt, Jonathan was giving over his authority to David and giving up his inherited right of succession to his father's throne. This was a breathtaking act of respect for a much younger person, but one whom Jonathan realized was the chosen leader.

By pledging his loyalty to David, Jonathan not only gave up his throne and career but also risked the wrath of his father, King Saul. He risked not only family relationships, but also His own life. This depth of loyalty is seldom seen in the church today, much less in the world.

Jonathan tangibly gave his best to see David come into the full purpose of God's anointing. Out of pure respect, Jonathan was a facilitator of God's best being brought into fruition for another, even to the point of sacrificing all that he could have claimed for himself.

Jonathan demonstrated the rare ability of balancing his priorities. He found a way to be loyal to the command to honor his father, to honor the laws of the land (and its wayward king), and to honor the supreme authority, God. In spite of all the risks, Jonathan stuck with his father, even to the point of ultimately dying with him in battle.

What did Jonathan see in David? What caused him to express such love and loyalty? He saw the one chosen by God. He saw a man after God's own heart. He saw not a perfect man, but one willing to be corrected. He saw one contrite and broken, generous and forgiving, anointed and humble. He saw one full of courage and endowed with uncommon valor.

LIVING THE LAWS

The church today desperately needs more Jonathans who will be so attuned to God's leading that they put Him first by putting others first. The person who lives by this Law of Heartful Humility is practicing the principle of Christlikeness: "Your attitude should be the same as that of Christ Jesus: Who, being in very nature God, did not consider equality with God something to be grasped, but made himself nothing, taking the very nature of a servant, being made in human likeness. And being found in appearance as a man, he humbled himself and became obedient to death — even death on a cross!"[6]

Seek an elevated purpose, not an elevated position.
Jonathan, the king's son, a victorious warrior and heir to the throne, made himself of no reputation, gave it all up and became a servant to the teenage shepherd boy, humbling himself even to the point of risking his life over and over again — so that the shepherd boy would come into his highest and best fulfillment of purpose and anointing. As stewards devoted to Jesus Christ, we too must seek an elevated purpose, not an elevated position.

Give and give up. Jonathan was willing both to give and to give up in order that God's will be done. He lovingly yielded his resources. He boldly intervened and interceded for David, knowing that the young man was God's chosen servant. He set aside his "rights" and sought the higher good. In all of these ways, Jonathan is an example to us as believers today. We, too, must be willing to give, and to give up, in order that God's will be accomplished. We, too, must intercede for those whom God has chosen to use in His service. We, too, must humbly seek the higher good.

Scripture References:
[1] 2 Corinthians 8:9
[2] John 3:30
[3] 1 Samuel 14:1
[4] 1 Samuel 18:1
[5] 1 Samuel 18:3-4
[6] Philippians 2:5-8

26

THE LAW OF
UNCONDITIONAL
CONTENTMENT

*The steward's contentment is not dependent
upon the steward's circumstances.*

A t one point, more than a hundred people were in line, patiently waiting their turn in spite of the biting cold. Blustery weather would not deter them from this opportunity and they were ready, money in hand. The convenience store had never done such a business, and on Christmas of all days! In fact, the store wasn't even supposed to be open, but the demand was so great that the owner himself was working the register. From morning to late afternoon the customers kept coming, some of them spending hundreds of dollars — and everyone was buying the same thing: a chance to win millions. In the end, only one lucky guy in another state held the winning ticket. Millions of others were left with worthless scraps of paper — the flimsy reminders of what might have been.

In the relentless pursuit of satisfaction, people have always chased dreams. They tell themselves, "If only I had more money (or a bigger house, or a better car, or a different job, or finer clothes) then I would be content." But, of course, they wouldn't be, because our natural bent as human beings is to constantly want something more than we already have. If we have a substantial amount of money it still doesn't seem like quite enough. If we live in a spacious house it still seems not quite big enough. If we drive a decent automobile we still look with jealousy at the better ones passing by. Satisfaction seems so hard to come by; yet we can experience it if we learn the Law of Godly Contentment. The Apostle Paul discovered this truth and it changed his perspective on everything: "I have learned to be content whatever the circumstances," he wrote. "I know what it is to be in need, and I know what it is to have plenty. I have learned the secret of being content in any and every situation, whether well fed or hungry, whether living in plenty or in want. I can do everything through him who gives me strength."[1]

When we consider the circumstances Paul was enduring when he wrote these words, our own struggles pale in comparison. He was in prison. Chained and restricted in a dank cell, he was unable to travel and minister freely. He was sick. A chronic illness kept him in relentless pain. He was abandoned. Many of his so-called Christian friends and brothers had turned against him. For reasons that are unclear, they had ceased their support, and many were actually attacking him with vicious criticism. Faced with similar woes, many people would become bitter. Some would become depressed and melancholic. Others would react with self-pity. Paul's response, however, was governed by the Law of Unconditional Contentment. In spite of all the things going against him circumstantially, his heart was not troubled.

The circumstances will get to every person at one time or another and we can find solace in the fact that Paul "learned" contentment. It did not come to him naturally. The word "learned" means "learned by experience." In other words, it happened in the context of life, not merely through some sort of intellectual process.

The word "content" has a fascinating definition: it means "contained." Paul had learned the containment of God in every dimension of his life, channeling him and controlling him. He was living a remarkable paradox: Even though he was physically bound in a Roman jail, his captors were not containing him and directing him; God was. Paul rested on the Lord's sovereignty and providence; and he had learned through his experiences to look at life not as a series of accidents but a series of appointments.

What is the secret to contentment in all circumstances? There are two elements to the equation. First, contentment comes through awareness of God's presence. Second, contentment comes through alertness to God's purposes. Paul was keenly aware of God's presence because it was the source of his peace. That is why he boldly told the Philippians, "Whatever you have learned or received or heard from me, or seen in me — put it into practice. And the God of peace will be with you."[2] Peace, in the spiritual sense, does not mean an absence of problems and hostilities. In fact, in this life conflict is a constant; but God's peace rules in our hearts and gives us the perfect resource in time of trouble. God allows us to go through tough times and even neglect, for in adversity and loneliness He can often teach us things we wouldn't otherwise learn. In spite of all his hurt, Paul was able to see God's hand in what was going on in his life. He was clued in to God's purposes.

LIVING THE LAWS

Place your confidence in Christ's control. Unconditional Contentment seems like such a lofty goal. But the fact is that it can become a normal state of life. The first step toward that ideal is to place your confidence in Christ's control. This is not a once-for-all expression of confidence, but a daily, even momentary declaration of faith. Then, like Paul, you can experience the power of that control whether things are up or down. When circumstances are negative, Christ controls and enables you to respond in a positive manner. When circumstances are positive, Christ controls and liberates you from the negative, selfish tendencies that can so easily derail our thoughts and attitudes.

Place your confidence in Christ's strength. The second step toward Unconditional Contentment is to place your confidence in Christ's strength. Paul knew that in his own inclinations, he was not fit for the circumstances he faced. However, relying on Christ's strength, he was able to consistently overcome the most daunting obstacles. As he said so succinctly: "I can do everything through him who gives me strength." The good news is that we, too, can know the satisfaction and joy of this same matchless strength. It is readily available, abundantly powerful and ours to receive.

Scripture References:
[1] Philippians 4:11-13
[2] Philippians 4:9

27

THE LAW OF
PASTORAL PROVISION

God's people must take care of God's servants.

H ave you ever tried to pat your head with your right hand while rubbing your tummy with the left? It's quite a challenge for a large percentage of the population! And for many Christians it's similar to being practical and spiritual at the same time: they struggle to get both motivations operating simultaneously. Some are so heavenly minded they're no earthly good, or vice versa. But this is not the way God meant things to be. His will, in fact, is that believers be both thoroughly spiritual and thoroughly practical. God matures us spiritually as we minister practically, and He achieves His divine ends through human means. A good example of this truth is the Law of Pastoral Provision which governs the practical care that Christians are to give their spiritual leaders. Paul explained it like this to Timothy: "The elders who direct the affairs of the church well are worthy of double honor, especially those whose work is preaching and teaching. For the Scripture says, 'Do not muzzle the ox while it is treading out the grain.' and 'The worker deserves his wages.'"[1]

Paul certainly knew the impact of this principle in his own life and ministry. He wrote about it to the Philippians: "As you Philippians know, in the early days of your acquaintance with the gospel, when I set out from Macedonia, not one church shared with me in the matter of giving and receiving, except you only; for even when I was in Thessalonica, you sent me aid again and again when I was in need." And he adds, "Not that I am looking for a gift, but I am looking for what may be credited to your account. I have received full payment and even more; I am amply supplied, now that I have received from Epaphroditus the gifts you sent."[2] At a crucial moment, Paul's needs were so great that he called them "an affliction." He was like a soldier out of contact with his unit, his ammunition depleted, his radio malfunctioning, his food supplies desperately low. He had a bonafide crisis, and he needed some fellow Christians to live by the Law of Pastoral Provision. Fortunately, that's exactly what the Philippians did. They shared with him at the point of his most pressing need, giving generously and sacrificially to provide life's necessities and alleviate his pain.

The fundamental nature of sharing is wrapped up in Paul's simple phrase, "giving and receiving." This reminds us of the instruction Jesus gave to His twelve disciples when He sent them out to preach the gospel of the Kingdom: "Freely you have received, freely give."[3] Sharing, at its core, is not related to personal inclination or applied pressure, but to the grace of God. He has graciously given to us, and we are to graciously give in return. Sharing is a response of loving obedience motivated by His goodness. When we do share, He gives even more and blesses in even greater measure.

Stewardship on behalf of spiritual leaders is a very important matter. The Scripture is clear that *God's people must take care of God's servants.* If we fail to do so, we risk "muzzling the ox" — preventing our servant-leaders from doing what God has called them to do. This responsibility is an ongoing priority which requires persistent giving and sharing, just as the Philippian believers did for Paul. The blessing, of course, ends up being a two-way street: what is given is "credited to your account" and its value greatly multiplied by God. If you have the slightest doubt about this, consider what Jesus said about those who give to His servants: "He who receives you receives me, and he who receives me receives the one who sent me. Anyone who receives a prophet because he is a prophet will receive a prophet's reward, and anyone who receives a righteous man because he is a righteous man will receive a righteous man's reward. And if anyone gives even a cup of cold water to one of these little ones because he is my disciple, I tell you the truth, he will certainly not lose his reward."[4]

It is more blessed to give than to receive. This is not some pithy saying from Reader's Digest. It's a biblical truth. The only way to lose is to fail to share. And even if we have to share out of our poverty, the blessing is certain. As we give, whatever our capacities, we are doing the will of God, and we give Him pleasure because He sees us becoming more like His Son.

LIVING THE LAWS

God ensures that the one who shares does not suffer because he shares. That's why Paul, immediately after commending the Philippians for their gift, states, "And my God shall meet all your needs according to his glorious riches in Christ Jesus."[5] What a reassuring fact this is, that God supplies according to His riches. The important phrase to notice in this promise is "according to." This is different from "out of." He blesses us "according to" the full measure of His wealth. It's like the difference between the billionaire who gives you his ATM card and says "use it as needed" versus the billionaire who says, "here's a $1000 gift to help you out." One gift is "according to" the riches; the other is "out of" the riches. God's blessings, thankfully, are always "out of" the richness of who He is, always perfectly compatible with His very being.

Be consistent, be persistent and be thankful toward your pastors. As you obey the Law of Pastoral Provision, be consistent, be persistent and be thankful toward your spiritual leaders. Share generously with them, knowing that they bear a great responsibility of oversight. "Remember your leaders, who spoke the word of God to you. Consider the outcome of their way of life and imitate their faith."[6]

Give more than money. In many cases, the best gift you can give to a pastor is not a monetary gift but some other expression of concern and appreciation. Among the gifts most prized by godly leaders are notes of encouragement, times dedicated to intercessory prayer for them, or books or resources to enrich their ministry.

Remember that some spiritual leaders are worthy of double honor. According to Paul's words to Timothy, those who are responsible for the public ministry of God's Word, whose main calling is preaching and teaching, are worthy of even more honor. That honor should be expressed in how we pay them, how we treat them, how we pray for them and how we encourage them to fulfill God's calling.

Scripture References:
[1] 1 Timothy 5:17-18
[2] Philippians 4:15-18
[3] Matthew 10:8
[4] Matthew 10:40-42
[5] Philippians 4:19
[6] Hebrews 13:7

28

THE LAW OF
GODLY CONTENTMENT

Wise stewards are happy with what they have,
not hassled by what they don't have.

Prisons today are five-star resorts compared to those in which Paul languished. He didn't have a heated cell with a private toilet and sink. There was no mattress on which to sleep, no TV room in which to relax, no well-stocked library for reading and study. There was only the dark encasement of roughly hewn stones, damp air filled with putrid odors and the pungent reminders of human depravity. Perhaps worst of all were the chains, their rusty coarseness scraping his skin raw, constantly tugging at him.

And, as if imprisonment were not painful enough, Paul had to endure the stinging criticism of those who called themselves his Christian brothers. They dared to attack God's apostle even while he was held captive.

Stop and imagine yourself in Paul's situation. Feel the weight of the chains on raw skin. Taste the nauseating swill that was his daily food. Listen to those dreadful sounds of suffering that filled his ears day and night. Look into the menacing eyes of the Roman prison guards.

You are there. You are suffering. You are chained. You are Paul the apostle. Now, what's your attitude? What fills your heart through the weary hours? Here's what Paul wrote to his friends in Philippi: "Now I want you to know, brothers, that what has happened to me has really served to advance the gospel. As a result, it has become clear throughout the whole palace guard and to everyone else that I am in chains for Christ. Because of my chains, most of the brothers in the Lord have been encouraged to speak the word of God more courageously and fearlessly."[1]

> When we finally depart this world we leave everything behind. Everything. Our properties, our vehicles, our furnishings, our bank accounts, the clothes in our closets — it's all left behind. When the moment of our departure comes, all that matters is what we've built up in spiritual riches.

What an attitude! Rather than being inflamed with furious self-pity, Paul is encouraged by the positive impact of his negative condition. In spite of the severity, he is joyful. What a lesson he teaches us! We have troubles and trials, sure; but what is our attitude, and what is our commitment? Paul was joyful and he kept on giving because he lived by the Law of Godly Contentment. He knew that he was just a pilgrim, and his affections were directed above, not below. From personal experience he could tell his brothers and sisters in Christ, "Set your minds on things above, not on earthly things."[2]

Wise stewards are happy with what they have, not hassled by what they don't have. "Godliness with contentment is great gain," Paul wrote in a letter to Timothy, "for we brought nothing into the world, and we can take nothing out of it."[3] When each of us arrives in our birthday suit we have nothing but a physical body. And, although we amass things throughout life, when we finally depart this world we leave everything behind. Everything. Our properties, our vehicles, our furnishings, our bank accounts, the clothes in our closets — it's all left behind. When the moment of our departure comes — as it certainly will — all that matters is what we've built up in spiritual riches.

LIVING THE LAWS

Be satisfied with life's essentials. It's easy in a culture of abundance to define "essentials" in a much broader sense than God ever intended. We should in fact think as simply as possible, being willing to be satisfied with food to eat, clothes to wear, and a place to live. For Paul, the essentials were even fewer. He wrote: "But if we have food and clothing, we will be content with that."[4] Being satisfied is not a struggle if one simply remembers the goodness of God. As the psalmist said, "He satisfies your desires with good things."[5]

Be wary of life's temptations. One of life's biggest temptations is money. We all want it, and most of us want a lot of it. But, as the Scripture reminds us, "the love of money is a root of all kinds of evil."[6] It can sidetrack us from God's core purposes and make us forget that His indwelling presence is our source. "Keep your lives free from the love of money and be content with what you have, because God has said, 'Never will I leave you; never will I forsake you.' So we say with confidence, 'The Lord is my helper; I will not be afraid. What can man do to me?'"[7]

Be happy in life's circumstances. Circumstances change constantly. We can go from delight to disaster in a single day. For the faith-filled believer, it really doesn't matter how things are going because confidence in the Lord transcends concern for the circumstances. Paul wrote from prison, "I have learned to be content whatever the circumstances. I know what it is to be in need, and I know what it is to have plenty. I have learned the secret of being content in any and every situation, whether well fed or hungry, whether living in plenty or in want."[8] The "secret" that Paul learned is that Christ enables us to be happy regardless of what is going on. He is the constant in a world of change. Through His empowerment we can live by the Law of Godly Contentment.

Scripture References:
[1] Philippians 1:12-14
[2] Colossians 3:2
[3] 1 Timothy 6:6-7
[4] 1 Timothy 6:8
[5] Psalm 103:5
[6] 1 Timothy 6:10
[7] Hebrews 13:6
[8] Philippians 4:11-12

29

THE LAW OF
FUTURE-FOCUSED GIVING

Wise stewards invest for the longest possible term.

I n an essay entitled *An Unclouded Vision*, best-selling author Chuck Swindoll lists several amusing quotations from men whose vision was clouded on some important subjects:

On World Population..."The population of the earth decreases every day, and, if this continues, in another ten centuries the earth will be nothing but a desert." Montesquieu, 1743

On Anesthesia..."The abolishment of pain in surgery is a fantasy. It is absurd to go on seeking it today. Knife and pain are two words in surgery that must forever be associated in the consciousness of the patient. To this compulsory combination we shall have to adjust ourselves." Dr. Alfred Velpeau, 1839

On Aviation..."The demonstration that no possible combination of known substances, known forms of machinery, and known forms of force can be united in a practical machine by which man shall fly long distances through the air, seems to the writer as complete as it is possible for the demonstration of any physical fact to be." Simon Newcomb, astronomer, 1903

On the Atomic Bomb..."That is the biggest fool thing we have ever done. The bomb will never go off, and I speak as an expert in explosives." Admiral William Leahy to President Harry Truman, 1945

Though well meaning, these men just didn't see things in the right way. They looked at the natural world and came to some very wrong conclusions. Of course, we shouldn't be too hard on them, because that's a problem common to human beings: we see reality through our own eyes rather than through God's. That was precisely the problem with a wealthy man who was the subject of a parable Jesus taught. We've considered his story before, but it bears a second look: "The ground of a certain rich man produced a good crop. He thought to himself, 'What shall I do? I have no place to store my crops.' Then he said, 'This is what I'll do. I will tear down my barns and build bigger ones, and there I will store all my grain and my goods. And I'll say to myself, "You have plenty of good things laid up for many years. Take life easy; eat, drink and be merry."' But God said to him, 'You fool! This very night your life will be demanded from you. Then who will get what you have prepared for yourself?'" Jesus then concluded: "This is how it will be with anyone who stores up things for himself but is not rich toward God."[1]

The rich man looked at his life and saw only himself, not God. He failed to remember that he was a steward to whom much had been entrusted. The fact that this farmer had such a rich harvest did not prove that he was in any way a better man. It simply showed that God was kind and gracious to him. Wealth, after all, is no measure of worth. The person who looks at himself and forgets God when blessings are abundant is gripped by pride and self-deceit. Moses certainly knew about this sinful tendency when he warned his people to prepare themselves for the blessings of the Promised Land. He was not sure they could handle the blessings as well as they could the battles and the burdens.[2]

The man in the parable had "I" trouble. His boastful statements are laced with personal pronouns for he instinctively thought only of himself. Rather than being humbled by his good fortune, he instead further inflated his ego. He felt so secure, not knowing he was in grave danger. Like many people today, he had the false notion that things can give peace, when in reality things more often create worry. Perhaps that's why Jesus preached a sermon on worry right after giving this parable. Worry is a sign of security placed in the wrong source. The worldly-minded person looks at material things and equates those things with security. Jesus challenged such thinking and warned against building a life on sand.

There is nothing wrong with being future-focused; indeed, the Law of Future-Focused Giving is a key precept of stewardship. It teaches us that *wise stewards invest for the longest possible term*. They think about the heavenly future, not the earthly. They enjoy things, but they do not depend upon them. They provide for the future, but they don't predict it. As Paul instructed Timothy, "Commend those who are rich in this present world not to be arrogant nor to put their hope in wealth, which is so uncertain, but to put their hope in God, who richly provides us with everything for our enjoyment.

Command them to do good, to be rich in good deeds, and to be generous and willing to share. In this way they will lay up treasure for themselves as a firm foundation for the coming age, so that they may take hold of the life that is truly life."[3]

LIVING THE LAWS

Concern yourself more with investment than enjoyment. If your peace is based on things and not on the will of God, you have a false peace. To stay in balance spiritually, think in terms of investment rather than enjoyment. The self-assured rich man was obsessed with enjoyment, not realizing that he was about to abandon all the things he expected to enjoy. He was revealed as a foolish and selfish man, and his life came to a sudden end. In similar fashion, many Christians live like fools because their concern is success in this world, and they are driven by a false sense of security.

Be rich toward God. The eyes see what the heart loves. If we love God and put His will first in our lives, then whatever material blessings we receive will only draw us closer to Him. By investing in things eternal, by giving with a future-focused mindset, we become rich toward God.

Scripture References:
[1] Luke 12:16-21
[2] Deuteronomy 6:10-12
[3] 1 Timothy 6:17-19

30

THE LAW OF
ABSOLUTE HARVEST

Sow sparingly, reap sparingly;
sow bountifully, reap bountifully.

I n civil law, changes occur constantly as legislators — our "lawmakers" — debate and devise and decide the standards that govern our lives. Laws come and go as society evolves.

In criminal law, changes occur with less frequency but they do happen. For example, capital punishment was for many years allowed by the law, then for years it wasn't, then again it was. Such shifts are common in a complex, democratic system.

In spiritual law, however, changes do not occur at all, for there is but one Lawmaker and He never changes. He is "the same yesterday, today and forever"[1] and His standards are fixed and permanent. Many of God's spiritual laws have a counterpart in the physical world, and none is more evident than the Law of Sowing and Reaping. According to this law, whatever is sown always determines what is reaped. If you sow corn, you'll reap corn, not wheat or beans or rice. It is impossible to reap something different from what one has sown. The same truth applies in the spiritual dimension. The Scripture teaches: "Do not be deceived: God cannot be mocked. A man reaps what he sows. The one who sows to please his sinful nature from that nature will reap destruction; the one who sows to please the Spirit, from the Spirit will reap eternal life. Let us not become weary in doing good, for at the proper time we will reap a harvest if we do not give up."[2]

There is an important corollary to the Law of Sowing and Reaping, an essential principle of stewardship which we can identify as the Law of Absolute Harvest. Paul expressed it this way: "Remember this: Whoever sows sparingly will also reap sparingly, and whoever sows generously will also reap generously."[3] We find this same truth in the ancient Proverbs of King Solomon, many centuries before the time of Christ. He wrote, "A generous man will prosper; he who refreshes others will himself be refreshed."[4]

The promise of absolute harvest is unalterable; it is totally in God's control. However, the decision as to what one sows is an individual decision. God doesn't force us to plant against our will; it's up to us to plant good seed and cultivate good crops in the soil of life. God's desire, clearly, is that we intentionally choose to plant and cultivate what is good, and to not give up in our well-doing. In daily stewardship this means consciously choosing to be generous, giving of ourselves and our resources without regard for the cost. This pleases our heavenly Father who ensures that the unwearied doing of good produces an unfailing harvest of good.

The effective steward is a fruitful steward, one whose life is filled with the fruits of righteousness. This bounty is described in many ways throughout the Bible. Paul called it "the fruit of the Spirit," which he defined as nine virtues: "love, joy, peace, patience, kindness, goodness, faithfulness, gentleness and self-control."[5] The power that produces this fruit is spiritual power, the power of Christ dwelling in us. As Jesus said of Himself, "I am the vine; you are the branches. If a man remains in me and I in him, he will bear much fruit; apart from me you can do nothing. If anyone does not remain in me, he is like a branch that is thrown away and withers; such branches are picked up, thrown into the fire and burned. If you remain in me and my words remain in you, ask whatever you wish, and it will be given you. This is to my Father's glory, that you bear much fruit, showing yourselves to be my disciples."[6]

To "remain" or "abide" in Christ is to live in obedience to His commands. As He said, "If you obey my commands, you will remain in my love, just as I have obeyed my Father's commands and remain in his love."[7] The Christian who does not abide in Christ does not please God, and his works will be burned at the judgment seat of Christ. This does not refer to losing one's salvation; it has only to do with the fruit of one's life. The day of Christ's judgment will bring to light the reality of that harvest. "It will be revealed with fire, and the fire will test the quality of each man's work. If what he has built survives, he will receive his reward. If it is burned up, he will suffer loss; he himself will be saved, but only as one escaping the flames."[8]

LIVING THE LAWS

The Law of Absolute Harvest is a truth that can clarify our thoughts and purify our motives. Remembering that we reap exactly what we have sown helps us to keep life in perspective and impels us to plant good seed at every opportunity. Bear in mind these priorities:

Sow generously not sparingly. God gives us a supply of "seed" to be planted for His purposes. Whatever He supplies to you, sow it generously and wisely. Don't waste your time or resources sowing seeds of unrighteousness because all you'll get is a crop of weeds. Sow with an abundant intensity and you'll reap abundantly.

Never give up in doing good. Sometimes Christians are mocked as "do-gooders." If it happens to you, let them mock, because you will be the winner; those who do good will reap a great harvest. Keep up the good work! Tenacity in well-doing is a sterling quality of stewardship.

Be patient. The spiritual harvest will come. It is a well-defined, well-ordered process that is in God's hands, not our own. Just as a physical crop comes in its own time and on its own terms, the spiritual crop cannot be rushed. We till the ground, we sow the seed, we cultivate the plants, but God gives the increase for He and He alone is Lord of the Harvest.

Scripture References:
[1] Hebrews 13:8
[2] Galatians 6:7-9
[3] 2 Corinthians 9:6
[4] Proverbs 11:25
[5] Galatians 5:22-23
[6] John 15:5-8
[7] John 15:10
[8] 1 Corinthians 3:13-15

31

THE LAW OF
SINGLE-MINDED SERVICE

One can serve God or serve money;
no one can serve both.

B ack in the heyday of radio no one was a bigger star than Jack Benny. His wry sense of humor resonated with millions of listeners every week on his wildly popular show. The main trait of the curmudgeonly character he played was stinginess. He was a man who simply would not part with his money. In one of his best-known comedy routines he is accosted by a robber who thrusts a gun into his chest and says, "Your money or your life!" Benny doesn't answer him and the flabbergasted robber says, "I said, your money or your life!" Finally, Benny replies, "I'm thinking...I'm thinking!"

Funny as that is, it seems to actually be that way for a lot of people. Money is so important to them that they value it above everything else. There's no question that money has an alluring power, tempting us with all that it can purchase or accomplish. If we give into it, we learn to our dismay that it has the power to control us and make us its servant. Jesus taught His disciples, "No servant can serve two masters. Either he will hate the one and love the other, or he will be devoted to the one and despise the other. You cannot serve both God and Money."[1]

In Jesus' teaching, the term "money" has a very broad meaning. It includes actual money, but it also includes everything to which we can become attached in this material world — all the things that money can buy. These are the "things of the world" which John cautions us not to love. In his first epistle he wrote, "Love not the world, neither the things that are in the world."[2] One well-known pastor suggested that a reasonable paraphrase of this verse for Christians in America would be, "Love not the mall, neither the things that are in the mall." To that we could all add a sincere, Amen! How well we know the temptations of money and the magnetic power it has in our culture; and how desperately we need to take to heart what Jesus said.

One of the most important principles of Christian stewardship is the Law of Single-minded Service. When we use the term *single-minded* it's obvious what we mean: having a single focus, a single interest, a single purpose. It implies exclusivity of devotion, a wholehearted commitment to God transcending all other commitments. Because of God's mercy and grace, this kind of commitment is our "reasonable service,"[3] as Paul told the Christians at Rome. We are to give ourselves as "living sacrifices," yielding unreservedly to the will of God.

Single-minded service requires several things of us as believers. It requires self-denial, the setting aside of personal wants. "If anyone would come after me," Jesus said, "he must deny himself and take up his cross and follow me."[4] Single-minded service also requires sacrifice. Those who choose the life of discipleship must give up personal ambitions for the sake of the Christ. "And he [Christ] died for all, that those who live should no longer live for themselves but for him who died for them and was raised again."[5] Single-minded service requires perseverance as well. The faithful steward sticks to the priorities and does not give up. This is a truly serious matter, as evidenced in what Jesus once told a man who was struggling to commit: "No one who puts his hand to the plow and looks back is fit for service in the kingdom of God."[6]

LIVING THE LAWS

The Law of Single-minded Service is an all-too-often neglected principle among Christians. How easily we become distracted by other interests, how readily we are drawn away by problems and concerns; and whenever that happens we get a divided mind, fragmented in multiple directions. Single-mindedness demands constant spiritual discipline. Living by this precept is not easy, but it is rewarding.

Be single-minded about God's Word. Do what Joshua did, meditating on the Word day and night, being careful to do everything written in it. The result of that in his life was a succession of victories and an influence that touched an entire nation. His single-minded devotion was clear to everyone. "But as for me and my household," he said, "we will serve the Lord."[7]

Be single-minded about God's will. By yielding wholly to the Lord, refusing to be conformed to the pattern of this world, the believer is transformed spiritually. The impact of this transformation is that we are "able to test and approve what God's will is — his good, pleasing and perfect will."[8]

Be single-minded about God's work. There's no getting around the fact that life is consumed with activity. Each of us has work to do every day, tasks that occupy our time and drain our energies. But through it all, the wise steward keeps a single-minded view of what's truly important: the work of God and the fulfillment of His purposes in us. In this sense, all work is sacred if it is done with a heart focused on eternity.

Scripture References:
[1] Luke 16:13
[2] 1 John 2:15
[3] Romans 12:1
[4] Mark 8:34
[5] 2 Corinthians 5:15
[6] Luke 9:62
[7] Joshua 24:15
[8] Romans 12:2

32

THE LAW OF
CHANNELED RESOURCES

Stewards are the channels of an endless, eternal supply.

I n the 1930s, at the opening of a disarmament conference, King George VI of England made an important speech which was broadcast via radio to millions of eager listeners. In the midst of his words, someone tripped over wires which had been stretched across the floor, tearing them loose and interrupting the signal. The chief engineer, seeing the crisis unfold, quickly grasped the loose wires in his bare hands, providing a conduit for the signal. For twenty minutes, the current literally passed through him while the King finished his speech. His hands were slightly burned, but through them the words of the King were communicated to countless people, who heard the speech clearly and distinctly. Without the engineer's courage and endurance, the King's message would have failed to reach its destination.

Like that quick-thinking engineer, we too are to be channels for the King. Not the King of England, but the King of Kings, the Lord of all creation. We are called by God Himself to be the channels of His love, His grace and His truth. As stewards, we are the conduits of an endless, eternal supply. As subjects in His Kingdom, we live by the Law of Channeled Resources, because He has chosen to work through human instruments to accomplish His purposes. There's a beautiful example of this principle put to practice in the Book of Acts, chapter 3. Peter and John were going to the temple one day at the time of afternoon prayer when they encountered a crippled man who asked them for money. The Bible says, "Peter looked straight at him, as did John. Then Peter said, 'Look at us!' So the man gave them his attention, expecting to get something from them. Then Peter said, 'Silver and gold I do not have, but what I have I give you. In the name of Jesus Christ of Nazareth, walk.'"[1]

Imagine what this man must have thought. He had been crippled since birth, permanently incapacitated, unable to move anywhere on his own. Someone had to carry him to the place where he begged every day from people going into the temple courts. Passing by this poor beggar were the most learned theologians and philosophers of his time. He was situated in front of a spectacularly beautiful building, surrounded constantly by earnest worshippers. Yet for all of this he was in no way better. Seeing Peter and John, he asked them for money, hoping for a small donation. As a lame beggar, his head was probably hung in self-pitying humility. Peter commanded him, "Look at us!" The command was for one purpose: to arouse a sense of expectation, to quicken the man's faith.

Peter's next statement must have come as a disappointment to the crippled man, but the let-down was only momentary. "I don't have any money for you," Peter said. He would not be dropping any silver or gold coins into the man's lap;

and the fact is, that wouldn't have solved his problem anyway. What the man wanted was not in fact what he needed. He was begging for financial help when he needed spiritual healing and physical deliverance. Peter commanded, "In the name of Jesus Christ of Nazareth, walk." Then, "taking him by the right hand, he helped him up, and instantly the man's feet and ankles became strong. He jumped to his feet and began to walk. Then he went into the temple courts, walking and jumping, and praising God." As you might imagine, this caused no small stir. "When all the people saw him walking and praising God, they recognized him as the same man who used to sit begging at the temple gate called Beautiful, and they were filled with wonder and amazement at what had happened to him."[2]

LIVING THE LAWS

When believers are used by God as channels of His resources, the impact is formidable. This is vital to remember as stewards, for we are conduits of His love, grace and power. This miracle recorded in Acts 3 is, in a certain sense, like a parable. It demonstrates the power of God to heal literally and completely, but it is also designed to illustrate people's need in symbolic form. What happens to your body is not nearly as important as what happens in your innermost being. The greatest work of healing and restoration that took place in the beggar's life was not physical but spiritual, and the same is true of every individual. In the practice of Christian stewardship we must manage all kinds of resources, but the purpose is always fundamentally spiritual.

Be an open channel. God wants to use you as vehicle through which to bring glory to Himself. Whatever He gives you in terms of resources is to be channeled, not dammed up and stored for personal benefit. The more open you are, the more blessed you will be.

Be an observant servant. It is crucial to be flexible, to be aware of people and their real needs. Peter could have easily said, "Old man, don't bother me. Can't you see I'm on my way to a prayer meeting?" But he didn't, of course, and the result was life-changing. As a follower of Christ, Peter and John knew to be observant and to expect interruptions and changed schedules. An important spiritual lesson in this is that we must be more people-oriented than goal-oriented.

Be objective about what matters to God. What is our objective as stewards? What are our goals? What really matters? When we get to heaven it will be vividly and pointedly clear: we will find only people in heaven. There will be no sermon notes, no committee memos, no study guides. People are the raw material of heaven, and we must love them as God Himself loves. How wise we are to remember what Jesus said: "As the Father has sent me, so send I you."[3] He was sent to do the Father's will, as we are. He was sent to communicate the Father's truth, as we are. He was sent to convey the Father's power, as we are. As stewards and servants, we must never forget these things.

Scripture References:
[1] Acts 3:4-6
[2] Acts 3:6-10
[3] John 20:21

33

THE LAW OF
LOVING COMPLIANCE

*Pure obedience prompted by pure love
produces pure stewardship.*

I n most translations of the Bible it's a relatively short verse. About 20 words or so. But in those words one can discover a virtual gold mine of theological truths and life-changing lessons. There is a richness of meaning that has indisputable value. At first reading, one might not be impressed with this brief sentence because it's an obituary of sorts.

Any day of the year we can open the local newspaper and read accounts of recent deaths. These accounts often include a flowery tribute to the deceased. But this obituary is different because it describes the death of One who was unique among all who have ever lived on this earth. This is the obituary of the one true God/Man...

"And being found in appearance as a man, he humbled himself and became obedient to death — even death on a cross!"[1]

Outwardly, Jesus appeared to be like any other man. When people looked at Him, they saw a man, not the

God/Man. There is often a difference between reality and the perception of reality. What others think to be real is frequently not what is actually there. Or, sometimes, they will see only one dimension. The reality is that Jesus Christ was not just 100% man but 100% God as well; but this truth can only be perceived through one means: the illuminating power of the Holy Spirit.

Jesus was by very nature, God. All that God is, Jesus Christ was, is and ever shall be. What can be said of the Son can be said of the Father and the Holy Spirit. The Father is God, the Son is God, and the Spirit is God; yet there is only one God. Jesus was not simply the most God-conscious man who ever lived, nor was He simply like God. He was, in fact, equal with God. His equality was total: all the attributes of God are true of Him. His equality was eternal. Even on earth, He claimed oneness with the Father. But Jesus "did not consider equality with God something to be grasped."[2] He didn't selfishly hang on to His rights as deity. Instead, He did something absolutely astounding: He humbled Himself.

Jesus' humility was self-motivated and self-induced. He was not humbled by others; He "humbled himself." These are completely voluntary acts, the willful submission of His will to the Father's will. When He prayed so passionately in Gethsemane's garden, His heart's cry was, "My Father, if it is possible, may this cup be taken from me. Yet not as I will, but as you will."[3] He was about to submit to the injustices of an unlawful arrest, an unfair trial and the vicious mockery of hateful people. But He went through all of it because of His matchless love, and we are the beneficiaries. "At just the right time, when we were still powerless, Christ died for the ungodly. Very rarely will anyone die for a righteous man, though for a good man someone might possibly dare to die. But God demonstrated his own love for us in this: While we were still sinners, Christ died for us."[4]

Why did Jesus come? A number of answers could be offered. He came to live a perfect life as our example. He came to suffer and die as our sacrifice. He came to conquer death as our resurrected redeemer. All of these things are true; however, they don't fully answer why Jesus came. The one over-arching reason is this: He came to do the Father's will. Doing what the Father willed included living a perfect life, dying a sacrificial death and rising again in redemptive power. But the essential, underlying answer remains: He came to do the Father's will. For us, this is very significant and it has a direct connection to our stewardship. Just as Jesus' purpose was to do the Father's will, so is ours. We can't live a perfect life or die a sacrificial death or rise again after our passing. But we don't need to because Jesus has already done it all and He has declared with authority, "It is finished!"[5] His saving work is done. But our serving work continues, because we are called to do the Father's will until our days are ended.

The final law of stewardship for our consideration is the Law of Loving Compliance. It's a principle incorporating genuine love and godly obedience. To be lovingly compliant is to do the will of God because you love Him and you want to obey Him explicitly. There's not an ounce of coercion involved. It's *pure obedience prompted by pure love which produces pure stewardship*. It's the essence of Christlikeness.

Jesus took on the nature of a servant — literally, a slave. As God, He was sovereign, deserving to be served. Yet He became a slave in order to fulfill the Father's purpose. His testimony is amazing: "By myself I can do nothing; I judge only as I hear, and my judgment is just, for I seek not to please myself but him who sent me."[6] In the stewardship of all the Father had entrusted to Him, He chose to demonstrate loving compliance.

LIVING THE LAWS

Pursue maturity, not perfection. As we endeavor to live by this standard, the Law of Loving Compliance, we cannot and will not achieve perfection. But we can achieve spiritual maturity, and that should be the priority. "Let us go on to maturity,"[7] the author of Hebrews wrote. Maturity in this sense means being grounded in the truth, for "we have this hope as an anchor for the soul, firm and secure."[8]

Yield the right of way. The good steward is a good servant, one whose rights have been yielded fully to the Lord. Such a servant claims ownership of nothing, but stewardship of all that God has given. Daily and deliberately, the trustworthy steward dedicates everything to Him alone.

Run with the finish line in view. In the race of life, don't grow weary or lose heart, because it's all worth it. "Therefore, since we are surrounded by such a great cloud of witnesses, let us throw off everything that hinders and the sin that so easily entangles, and let us run with perseverance the race marked out for us. Let us fix our eyes on Jesus, the author and perfecter of our faith, who for the joy set before him endured the cross, scorning its shame, and sat down at the right hand of the throne of God."[9]

You have a race marked out for you by God Himself. As a faithful steward, run strong and keep your eyes on the finish line. The One you serve is waiting there, ready to say, "Well done, good and faithful servant."

Scripture References:
[1] Philippians 2:8
[2] Philippians 2:6
[3] Matthew 26:39
[4] Romans 5:6-8
[5] John 19:30
[6] John 5:30
[7] Hebrews 6:1
[8] Hebrews 6:19
[9] Hebrews 12:1-2